The Human Herd

ADVANCE PRAISE FOR
THE HUMAN HERD

"In these challenging and disorientating times, Beth Anstandig is the person you want in the arena with you. Her smart insights, instinctual wisdom and life experiences are profound. Her book promises to be valuable for both our personal and professional lives. By encouraging us to pause, she'll help us to be more in touch with the animal within and create the space we need to make sense of things and make smart decisions."

—**Alison van Diggelen**, BBC Contributor
Host of *Fresh Dialogues*

"Beth Anstandig's work delivers the reader into the heart of Natural Leadership with ease and grace. Page after page she gently reawakens our innate understanding of what it means to be part of a community that shares a common mission. Here she has masterfully woven lessons from her life experience, her unbridled love of nature, and her academic training into a model that reminds us how to lead in an authentic, inspiring, and effective way. She paves the way for each of us to reconnect with our ability to build trust, safety, inspiration, and respect within our team. If you are interested in unearthing the natural leader within yourself, I highly recommend you take a deep breath, settle in, and read this book."

—**Maggie Merritt**, Executive Director, Steinberg Institute

"If you were a child who stared into animals' eyes and knew they could speak to you, you were right. This book is for all of us who tried to talk to animals as children, because we knew they had something to teach us."

—**Sam Lamott**, Podcast Host, *How to Human*
Owner, Hello Humans

"I wish Beth wrote this book years ago. I've been on a deep dive into unravelling my stuff, and this book joins the dots of everything I've been looking into. Beth brings her experience as a therapist and as a horsewoman and combines them into a book that will help a lot of people on their journey to discovering their true selves."
—**Warwick Schiller**, Podcast Host, *The Journey On*

"Well into my self-development journey, Beth has written the book that brings it all together for me. A lifelong animal owner and lover myself, Beth shines a light on why I'm more myself with them than any human. She gives us a pathway to find our way back to our authentic selves with her engaging stories and practical tools and exercises."
—**Robyn Schiller**, World Champion Equestrian

"The moment my eyes fixated on the first word and my mind began to process the stories, I was immediately swept away on a journey full of sensory stimulation and deep introspection. Beth's ability to seamlessly fuse narrative, descriptive and technical writing styles into this brilliant and practical masterpiece is striking. Beth's experiences quickly become the reader's experiences by very nature of the amount of colorful detail Beth provides. You feel as if you are in the moment with her. But even more captivating is Beth's ability to draw the reader into a place of recollection of one's own moments of vulnerability, personal exploration, and spiritual growth. For anyone looking to lead with more conviction, authenticity, vulnerability, and empathy, this book will get you there. For anyone looking to better serve the people around you, this book will get you there. For anyone looking to discover your voice and show up as your most genuine and uninhibited self, this book will get you there. For anyone seeking a true awakening of your fullest leadership potential, turn the page and join Beth on the journey. *The Human Herd* will get you there."
—**Karrah Herring**, Chief Equity Officer, State of Indiana Governor Eric J. Holcomb

"For those of us who are communicators for a living, this is a must-read. We spend so much time stressing to put the right words together to tell people what we want them to know. But so, so, so often we forget about what people actually need to hear and how they need to hear it, especially when times are tough. As Beth reminds us, *'Our cities are crowded, our schedules are overbooked, our workplaces are stifling. These unforgiving elements take a toll and our inner animal retreats in order to protect itself.'* In a world full of noise, Beth looks us square in the eye and challenges us to strip down our manmade defenses to form better connections within ourselves and with others."

—**Megan Hakes**, Crisis Communications Expert
Founder, H.PR Strategies

"This book will crack open your inner human-animal soul. It's an intimate look from a brilliant and transparent mind at how we can be our deepest selves, a roadmap set to poetry and words drawing out of oneness into something more alive: natural-born leadership! The first time through is gripping. It may seem like just reading about what's possible, and a rediscovery of self-awareness through relatable stories told beautifully enough so anyone can understand why these same lessons apply not just about leadership, but life."

—**Bryan Kramer**, Forbes Columnist, CEO H2H, Podcast Host
of *Humanly Possible*, TEDTalker

"Natural Leadership has offered me both a focused lens in which to view the world as well as concrete tools that I can rely on and apply in any situation or relationship. The steps that Beth walks you through are immediately relevant and applicable in any life circumstance. But the learning she offers is not just intellectual. She weaves her personal experience with vivid imagery and story that renders a deep visceral resonance. From the first stories she shares, you sense a shared knowing. I attribute this to our 'mammal bodies' and the collective experience that resides in our mammal DNA. But what is most compelling about Natural Leadership is Beth herself. She completely embodies Natural Leadership. Bearing witness to how she lives her life is the true testimony of the power of Natural Leadership."

—**Amy Hublou**, M.A., M.F.T., Founder, Imagine That Farm

"During these times when the world has become so disconnected, and the crucible of the pandemic has created energies that are rippling through our world, we must empower ourselves to refine our skills and reconnect to our Humanness. *The Human Herd* provides such an opportunity and indeed awakens us all to pay attention to the stirrings of our dormant selves. We know the work that needs to be done even as we fear it. As one willing to be willing, I continue to practice Natural Leadership in my personal and professional life. I have been reintroduced to the wilderness within and found the critical connection to my own humanity."

—**David P. Hott**, Director of Operations, Loaves and Fishes

"As someone with a lifelong involvement with horses, a lover of animals and nature, this book gives powerful insight and tools into how we as humans can tap into our animal bodies and awaken our authentic and Natural Leadership. Beth does a wonderful job at articulating how awareness within ourselves, others, and our environment can help us dig deeper into relationship and meaning. The stories helped me relate, the concepts brought it home, and the exercises created change. Utilizing the Natural Leadership model has helped me establish healthy boundaries with friends and family, helped me be a better manager by leveraging scope and feel within coaching relationships, and most importantly, helped me vocalize and connect with my needs."

—**Samantha Zorn**, Program Facilitator for
People Development, Google

"So many of us are living life in the passenger seat. On autopilot. Beth's work and this book is a call to arms to get in the driver's seat—stop living life by default and live by design. Beth speaks to each of us of the need for self-preservation whilst also providing us with a manual for how to in a beautiful and deeply relatable way."

—Kim Havens and Noa Ries, Co-founders of Kahilla

"What profound words to compassionately nurture our internal natures. As a fellow rider and wounded healer, I can appreciate Beth's parallels between the visceral experience of connection with nature and the clinical application of Natural Leadership to heal. A palatable explanation of neuroscience intertwined with the human experience, *The Human Herd* evokes a process exploring our innermost relationships with how we manifest the human animal to the world."

—Bryan Nguyen, M.A., M.F.T.
Director Outpatient Services, The Meadows

"In *The Human Herd*, Beth Anstandig invites the reader to embrace the sensations of the natural world, to build trust and connection with self and others, and to listen to our innate human signals of physical being through the practice of self-awareness. Chapter by chapter, she offers a guided journey through mammalian lessons on relationship, culture and community as a means for cultivating a practice she calls Natural Leadership. Her writing style is simultaneously raw and poetically inviting. Anstandig weaves humanizing stories with experientially grounded theory to form an approach to leadership that is both inclusive and accessible. Each page delivers provocative insights, relatable practices, and poignant reminders that are immediately impactful and enduringly transformative."

—Carol Ann Gittens, PhD, Dean of the Kalmanovitz School of Education at Saint Mary's College of California

THE HUMAN HERD

Awakening Our Natural Leadership

BETH ANSTANDIG

NEW YORK
LONDON • NASHVILLE • MELBOURNE • VANCOUVER

THE HUMAN HERD
Awakening Our Natural Leadership

Published in New York, New York, by Morgan James Publishing. Morgan James is a trademark of Morgan James, LLC. www.MorganJamesPublishing.com

Proudly distributed by Ingram Publisher Services.

ISBN 9781631956935 paperback
ISBN 9781631956942 ebook
Library of Congress Control Number:
2021941939

Cover Design & Graphics by:
Beth Brant
beth@bethbrant.com

Interior Design by:
Chris Treccani
www.3dogcreative.net

Cover Photo by:
Cassie Green Photography

Morgan James is a proud partner of Habitat for Humanity Peninsula and Greater Williamsburg. Partners in building since 2006.

Get involved today! Visit MorganJamesPublishing.com/giving-back

For Emma,
whose wholeness has inspired me to lead and love
with my truest self.

TABLE OF CONTENTS

"May we learn to return
And rest in the beauty
Of animal being,
Learn to lean low,
Leave our locked minds,
And with freed senses
Feel the earth
Breathing with us."
JOHN O'DONOHUE

ACKNOWLEDGMENTS

The animals have always been my teachers. This book is full of their lessons. These are their stories and concepts as much as they are mine. I hold in the highest regard the honor and the challenge of putting words to the animal experience so that the human herd can benefit.

Thank you to my daughter, Emma, whose early childhood words built a most generous bridge between the nonverbal mammal world and the complex landscape of human language. Our children have a lot to tell us about wellness if we are open enough to listen.

The Natural Leadership model integrates wisdoms from several disciplines I have studied and practiced during the last thirty years. As such, the classrooms in which I have learned have stretched beyond the universities where I earned degrees and into horse barns, sheepherding fields, meditation circles, the rooms of recovery, consultation groups, and therapist couches, just to name a few. I have had many beloved teachers who were resilient enough to endure my many questions and brave enough to ask me the questions I needed to answer. I would like to thank: Dr. Teri Quatman, Monica Stone, Dr. James Maddock, Dr. Noel Larson, Cynthia McReynolds, Nicky Riehl, Bill Berhow, Leslie Pfardresher, Billy Martin, Dee Dee Scott, Laura Gomez, Pam Lighfoot-Connor, Jill Muth, Jeanine Savard, Lori Carter, Venerable Suchart Siritool, Venerable Ekkasak Aggasakko, and Tami

Thompson. A special thanks to Jonathan Fishman for partnering in a human herd experience that has restored my sense of ease.

I would like to acknowledge Susan McCusker who co-founded The Circle Up Experience with me and helped me to see that my work was ready to leave a traditional psychotherapy setting.

I am grateful to the extraordinary editing talents of Jamey Jones who has taken such good care of my writing. Thank you to David Hancock and Morgan James Publishing for being inspired by this book, for trusting my vision for it, and for empowering me to publish it.

Finally, to those who I have had the great privilege of supporting, you have allowed me into your life and your inner world. Thank you for the gift to learn and develop alongside you.

INTRODUCTION
How We Settle In

We enter the sanctity of our being in the simplest moments—while playing with animals and watching birds fly, or standing in the dark awash with the shimmer of the moon, or watching a loved one wake into their truth. These uncluttered openings are the bare bones of grace.

MARK NEPO

This is the first, the wildest and the wisest thing I know: that the soul exists and is built entirely out of attentiveness.

MARY OLIVER

My heel catches the edge of the running board as I swing my legs out of the truck, held hostage by the narrow skirt squeezing my thighs. I shift out of the seat and try not to spill to the ground. I've compressed myself in so many ways today; I swear these pointed-toe heels will take me down. But right now, they raise me up and lengthen my stride. It's like I become another body, someone with stately legs and fingers like willows. Someone who knows the right thing to say and what to do with her hands. Only an hour earlier, I stood in the closet dreading another fancy party. Feeling desperate and lost, I chose the heels like a punishment for not fitting the mold. A deep longing from my bone marrow surfaced, a primitive reflex: Show up. Fit in. No matter what. I brushed off the dust and dog hair and shoved my feet inside, toes numbing almost instantly. I steamed and ironed the wrinkles of my garments and my being, buttoned up and quieted my oddities—so many contortions and folds as I collapsed into myself like a card table.

Yet again, I've painted myself into this familiar corner. One part of me is wild and free and knows her needs. She's the one who drives the truck, bought the ranch, and lives with a pack of dogs. She lies in the dirt with her horse herd, barefoot, dreaming up new ideas and poems. She can hear beyond words. But she's scared and sometimes finds herself too far out in front and alone. The Buddhist nun, Pema Chödron, says that anxiety is the human response to wide open space. The freedom to just be becomes too vast to bear. It's the panic a newborn feels unswaddled, a state of formlessness, without boundaries, an abyss of self. The other part of me is in that corner. She is tidied up, polished, and poised. She wears education and privilege like a designer bag, full of cash, connections, and credentials. She uses charm, irony, and an occasional sharp tongue as she chitchats her way through the country club lobby. But she's trapped, she can't breathe, and she's dying inside.

We hurry along the circular driveway with its tightly trimmed shrubbery and leafless sidewalks. Golf carts whir in the distance over an eerily silent backdrop that only an exclusive membership can buy. Every car is new and spotless. Every parking spot amply wide. No dents, no deviations, no signs of people coming or going or living. It seems fixed in time like artificial turfgrass or starched shirts that stand on their own. I've done this walk a thousand times, wrestling with these misaligned parts of myself. But this time it's different. There's a little girl holding my hand: Emma.

My daughter's sticky fingers twist along my wedding ring as we hurry across the hot asphalt. She's four years old and chatty— more than I could ever have imagined. The soundtrack to my life is her diminutive voice, flute notes fluttering the octaves. She narrates the day passing, the wind blowing, the emotions rising and falling as they do. She comments on her interior world, and she wants to know about mine. She weaves our emotional worlds together like a cloth she grasps, and she asks me to do the same. Today is different though. Today, she has worry in her throat, longer pauses between questions, something in her that hesitates. It has no name. Not yet.

We walk past the doorman, and she pulls my hand. She wants to look him up and down, wants to look in his face and figure him out. It's puzzling, this man who does nothing more than open and close a door. I have no words for her. We stitch the moment together with our eyes, our place of shared awareness, the gaze where we meet and know and breathe. This is the soft feel of our relationship, an invisible give-and-take that allows us to move through the world together. But I can feel my muscles constrict and my skin tighten. It's like I'm wearing a suit made of concrete. I can move, but only an inch or two before I hit the hard edges, the strict form that tells me I can't go any further and to stop being who I am. I hurry us forward, pulling her hand as I feel her willingness drag along the polished floors. When we get to the entrance of the banquet room, we both pause. The doorway busts at the seams—not with people but with pressure.

This time Emma yanks on my arm with force. We feel the increase in pressure at the same time, and we balk like animals startling and spinning toward safety. It's too much. I drop to my knees instinctively. Maybe prayer is this simple: the moment when you are at eye level with your child and you're humble and open enough to listen to the world through her pristine awareness, her unfiltered self-preservation. It's all I know to do. Feel the pressure. Stop. Listen.

It's been a lifelong standoff between me and pressure. But this time, I can't bulldoze through it. I can't small-talk it away with a mimosa in one hand and my daughter in the other. When I quit drinking, the mindless chatter and half-asleep social niceties became as painful as the three-day hangovers I gladly gave up.

We stop, and we stay. We stay at the banquet room entrance, Emma in her flowing party dress and me on my knees next to her. From her perspective, I can see a wall of looming lower body parts, distorted like when peering into funhouse mirrors. The tables are all pub height with crisp linens like satin ball gowns. We see a mix of chair legs and human legs, skin and stockings, metal and wood, some parts moving and others not. And there's so much noise. Laughter and talking. Joyful on the surface, but right below the celebratory hum the pressure builds like a thick patch of fog, a pocket of warm air, or an angry glare you wouldn't dare to pass. Emma squeezes my hand. I know.

She whispers, "I need a few minutes to settle in."

It's the wisest thing I've ever heard.

"Yes," I say. "I do too."

We stay there as if we're invisible. The party goers arrive around us: strangers, friends, family. We're like a rock formation in the middle of a river, the water moving around us, over us. It's the first time I've let myself stay put, to settle into a new space before trying to function or interact. Emma asked for what she needs, and it's what I need. It's what I've always needed. But I had built a life out of forgotten needs and ignored desires. I had been living under an anvil of pressure driven by internal expectations and external demands. Pressure that often became painful and left me feeling breathless, lifeless, and motionless.

The only way to live like that, with pressure, overwhelm, and pain, is to go numb. I had a thousand ways to stay busy or to chase accomplishments, to run from myself. I was half asleep at the wheel of my own life. Numb or wanting to be numb. I noticed opportunities for waking up pass me by from time to time, like a fog light scanning through the opaque night sky, one beam of clarity passing through darkness. My inner alarm clock would go off, but I just kept pressing snooze.

I was caught in a self-made trap, either chasing numbness or running to catch up with what I had missed while numbing out. I worked myself to the bone trying to be good enough, smart enough, successful enough, refined enough, succumbing to other people's expectations or stories about my identity that I had written and labeled as Truth. Then, in a dangerous mix of exhaustion and entitlement, I would free-fall wildly in the other direction, and the only way to get relief was to lose my mind. I did that with any behavior that could change my feelings or help me to not feel them at all. There was no middle path. It was all or nothing. I didn't work with the pressures of life, learning how to cope or choosing for myself how I wanted to live. Instead, I reacted.

By the time I became a parent, I had already bounced around rock bottom like it was a trampoline. Years of running from myself ended when I finally got sober. The emotional and spiritual blood flow returned to my limbs slowly but with a biting pain like after frostbite. Waking up is shocking. It's like leaving the movie theater after a matinee, opening the doors, and looking into the afternoon sky without sunglasses. It's blinding and disorienting, and nothing feels right. It's when we finally get in contact with ourselves—our feelings, sensations, the real stuff of our humanity—like a new layer of skin touching the air for the first time. For me, I've had to fully own my sensitivities, to see them as my most essential gifts, and to learn to take care of them in the grossly overstimulating world in which we live.

My animals have always been my teachers, my most gentle guides, showing me a way back to my vibrant and alive animal body. They have created a place of psychological safety from my earliest memories. I spent hours in a whelping box with litters of puppies when I was a baby, toddler, and a developing girl. The dogs and the horses insisted I meet them where they live: in the present, in honesty, and in the body. I needed them for this. I still need them. They ask me to stay in relationship with my truest self. Every day. Our children do the same. Just think of little Emma and how much honesty and directness she embodied in that moment when she expressed her needs so simply to me. Free of the layers of thought, judgment, and she knew exactly what she needed. I've built a life with the animals at the center of it so I can continue listening to the voice of my own animal, reclaiming the mammalian signal system that is alive and well within each of us.

When people come to our ranch to visit—to connect with themselves, to form better connections with each other, to learn, to heal, or to wake up—we start with this practice of Settling In, Emma's creation. The instruction is to take your animal body for a fifteen-minute walk and to explore the new environment. Visitors are encouraged to do exactly what their body wants and needs, to notice what they notice, and to follow their natural curiosity wherever it takes them. It's a freedom and honesty that so many people haven't had since childhood, one adults rarely give themselves (See "Take Your Animal Body for a Walk" in Chapter One).

Emma's simple lesson about Settling In teaches us to be aware of pressure and attend to it, teaching us how a slight adjustment can make a profound difference in how we take care of ourselves. This story was one of my most powerful awakenings into this radical and fundamental form of self-care, attending to our Natural Leadership. The story is yours now too. It's your invitation back to the primary part of yourself, an ever-present instrument of awareness that is your most trustworthy guide. This book is an invitation back into the world of the human animal, back into the world of you.

Let's settle into this space together, dear human animal reader. This is an invitation to you to awaken your exquisite sensitivity, to learn how to care for it, and to become inspired to use it as a guide in all that you do. Awareness of your sensitivity is a superpower. Perhaps it feels like a secret. It's not. It's the mammal part of you that is right there, just waiting for you.

Our Roadmap

One of my most beloved teachers and mentors, the late Dr. Jim Maddock, psychologist and theoretician, taught me a question that changed my life: What's happening right now? It seems too simple to be helpful, but it's a magic meta question that instantly creates the space we need to make sense of things. It helps us to orient ourselves in the world so that we can discern between our internal experience (mind, body, spirit, emotions) and the external world (the input from others and our surroundings). It's like pumping the brakes on our emotional or reactive brain so that our cognitive, meaning-making brain can catch up.

I've used Jim's question dozens of times a day for many years, and its value has deepened. Yet I noticed along the way that I needed a bit more from the question, as if there were a part of me I couldn't access with that one question alone. I live with a herd of horses, my teachers, and I spend long hours in the pasture with them, in their home, grazing alongside them, and learning their way of life, state of being, and patterns in relationships. As prey animals, they have a culture of interdependency, their roles and needs shifting through the herd all day, every day, every season, and in all life cycles. The core value of the herd is that they are better together. After all, safety in numbers makes the most sense for prey animals. To live in close proximity, sharing needs and roles, they have created and committed to an ongoing feedback system that is low-drama, ever-present, direct, and efficient.

The lessons they offer and the gentleness with which they teach I have yet to find in a human-led classroom. And I'm a lifelong learner with a few higher degrees! The herd, and my trusted pack of Border Collies, have shown me the way of Natural Leadership. They have asked that I loosen my grip on my human constructs, my limited world of ideas and insights, so that I can coexist with them. Animals are always honest. And because they are so very connected to needs as the basis of survival, they give us authentic feedback about what is needed in any given moment. They feel it when I show up with a socialized self that suppresses pressure instead of adjusting to it. They sense it when I've been afflicted by what I call The Busy Disease when I show up in their herd with too fast a pace. Their undeniable feedback comes in the form of body language and energy: tail swishes, a back leg raised asking for space, calming cues like yawning or laying down, moving away from confusion or pressure, or herding and cutting off movement when things have become dysregulated. They certainly communicate, with each other or with me, when things feel off or when adjustments are needed.

During those long hours with the herd, I would ask Jim's magic question to help me become more aware of what was happening in any given moment. I began to wonder about the awareness these animals need in order to survive. They may not be conscious or making thoughts, but awareness and alertness are fundamental to survival. As I walked alongside them, I began to notice what I have now named the Four Channels of Awareness (See Chapter Two).

Me. One, they must be attuned and attending to their individual needs, and in so doing, they are the finest teachers of self-care.

You. Two, they must sense the internal world of their herd mates, using a vast empathy system so that they can quickly respond when an individual senses danger.

Us. Three, in order to live together and have a reasonable amount of peace, they must tune in to the relationships in the herd, shaping and adjusting to proximity and resources as needs shift.

Environment. Four, they must be aware of their surroundings, picking up on the presence of anything new and assessing for safety.

These Four Channels of Awareness began to open for me as I spent time with the herd. With access to a vaster awareness, important elements of the Natural Leadership framework began to emerge.

A lot of people think that animals are the healers. This is a tough one for me. On the one hand, my animals saved my life and gave me a safe place to relate when I couldn't find one in childhood. There is no doubt they have helped and healed me along the way. They still do. On the other hand, I have come to realize that animals show us a pristine and fully intact part of ourselves, as mammals. That human animal part of us does not need to be fixed. It was never broken. It just needs a seat at the table. It wants us to listen to it. To see it.

The concepts of Natural Leadership are based on our innate signal systems as mammals and on phenomena that occur in the natural world. Our rich and brilliant human minds have the capacity to create and solve for seemingly impossible complexities. Our minds are responsible for remarkable innovation, necessary evolutions in how we live and relate. Yet our thinking brain is also the cause of great suffering. It creates a glitch in our survival system that bypasses how we take care of ourselves. We can think our way out of attending to real signals about our basic needs. We can believe thoughts that aren't true. After a traumatic event, our thoughts of shame and judgment can cause us to suppress our need to move and feel, resulting in illnesses like PTSD. We can become so lost in thought, language, and intellect that we don't even notice the basics of our well-being.

Let's be clear. It is not that this model of Natural Leadership suggests we subjugate the power of our minds. Rather, the model aims to inspire the human herd to integrate the wisdom of our mammal awareness so that our intellect and instincts can work in conjunction and in harmony. If we live, lead, and love empowered by Natural Leadership, we awaken a spirited and energizing part of our humanity that we need now more than ever before.

I also need to recognize my own deficiencies. While Natural Leadership is inherently inclusive and transcends the many hierarchies we humans have constructed, it's impossible for me to have a completely inclusive point of view because I only have *my* point of view. I do my best, but there is no way to do it perfectly. I cannot escape the system I live in. I do want us to view these concepts with as universal a lens as we can muster, all while recognizing our limitations. This book is about culture and relationships and is written from my vantage point. It is my hope that you will apply these concepts from your own life experiences and point of view.

How to Use This Book

In this book, you will encounter stories that illustrate the powerful lessons from nature and from the animal world. Whether you are an animal lover or not, the narratives will bring to life the core concepts of Natural Leadership. In each chapter, I will follow the story with an explanation and description of the concepts. I will also offer some practical tools and practices you can use, applying Natural Leadership to your world so that you can begin to use these powerful parts of yourself in everyday life.

Together, we will work on expanding awareness and scope, just like the horses, so that we have more information to work with and can make more strategic choices in how to lead ourselves and others. We will tune in to the phenomenon of pressure so that we can sense and adjust to it before we become flooded and overwhelmed. We will explore how to use pace so that we can conserve energy and shift our speed at the right times. We will look at naturally occurring motivators like the rhythms of the day or how we are drawn away from or driven toward others, and we will discover how we can use those forces. We will study how to shape relationships and create feedback systems in the groups we inhabit based on psychological and physical safety. We will look at how groups, teams, families, and communities can use Natural Leadership principles and practices to live in more interdependent human herds.

Culture Is About Behavior

As we go on this Natural Leadership journey together, it's important that we are intentional about the language we use. Culture, as a word, is loaded with meaning in the human world and often points to racial and ethnic identity. For animals, culture is remarkably basic and more attentive to survival. Group cultures are defined by the rules and norms of how individuals treat each other. Even animal groups have basic values, and their actions reflect those values. My horse herd, as an example, values togetherness, shared resources, peace, low to no drama, and emotional stability. As a result, the tone and texture of the herd animates those qualities. Humans can gain quick and accurate information about their cultures by paying attention to how they behave rather than what they say or think about their culture. Natural Leadership is inherently inclusive. Humans are meant to live together and are interdependent. Natural Leadership doesn't only apply to those at the top of the organizational chart. Anyone, in any position, anywhere can put it to use. It's a form of leadership that comes from the inside rather than being imposed from the outside and can be used within and between any group, no matter the race, ethnicity, class, or gender.

Leadership Is Relationship

Keeping our definition of leadership simple allows more emphasis and focus on relationships. Leadership is defined as: how each individual leads their life, takes care of self needs, and shows up in interactions with others, regardless of rank, title, or hierarchy. We lead ourselves all day, every day. When we think of ourselves as the leaders of our own lives, the concepts and lessons about leadership can be incredibly helpful and grounding. Whether we have a leadership title or not, we are also leading others. Parents are leading their children through the process of development. Teachers are leading classrooms. Coaches are leading their clients or teams toward growth. Spouses and partners lead each other to grow emotionally. Friends lead each other as they take turns offering support, suggesting activities, or pursuing creative endeavors.

The Powerful Pain of Rock Bottom

I am writing these words during what I have often called The Great Pause. Our global community has experienced a physical and mental health crisis like no other. With lockdowns and quarantines and social distancing, our lives are constricted beyond recognition by a viral pandemic. The pain, fear, and heartache of 2020 put inconceivable pressures on our families, work teams, neighborhoods, schools, medical systems, first responders, and social services. The Busy Disease was the precursor to COVID-19. It numbed us with to-do lists, errands, the activity shuffle, blind ambition, greed, the more-more-more, and the better-better-better. We were moving so fast that we didn't know our pace was heading down an unsustainable path.

We needed a rock bottom to wake up a necessary part of our humanity. And so, a virus woke us up. It sharpened all of our senses and snapped us back into a deeper layer of our animal awareness, a wild but wise part of us. The presence of this virus brought us back to our mammal bodies, to a deep connection to survival, safety, movement, our space, outdoors, animals, and the delicate nature of our health. It has also terrified us and forced us to experience present traumas and come to terms with past patterns of social trauma. The strain of living in isolation and fear has flushed out terrible injustices and imbalances in our family systems, political landscapes, and race relations.

We didn't know we were half asleep. We are only beginning to see. We are still waking up. And the waking up has been excruciating for so many. Disorienting. Devastating. Life-threatening. We have much to learn to rebalance and repair so that we can offer more to each other, to our children, and to ourselves. Let's walk through this together, human herd. We need each other.

Let's Practice

In this moment, give yourself some time to Settle In. Yes, right now while you are reading. Why not start this journey together with a new experience? Give yourself a reverent pause, a place in time to *just be.* However long you need or want. Better yet, give yourself both. Attend to your needs *and* your desires. Slow down.

Slow down even more. Breathe into your skin and bones. Feel your emotions in your belly. You might need to take some extra breaths to help your belly relax. Now, notice the ways you guard your heart. Hold your heart with your hands if you need to. Breathe some more. Consider that you might be able to soften and how your body might be able to let go of some pressure and tension.

Consider how a book about your mammal instincts, the wisdom of your nervous system, and your ancient wiring might serve you well. Consider what life might be like if you could hear the honest whispers of your needs and you could answer them. Breathe into that.

Consider that you know exactly what you need. Consider that you always have.

All of the messages are right there, just below the surface of thought and language.

This part of you has been dormant but is ready to wake up.

You are a human animal.

Let's begin.

CHAPTER ONE

Mammals

No matter where we are, the shadow that trots behind us is definitely four-footed.

CLARISSA PINKOLA ESTES

One often hears a horse that shivers with terror, or of a dog that howls at something a man's eyes cannot see, and men who live primitive lives where instinct does the work of reason are fully conscious of many things that we cannot perceive at all. As life becomes more orderly, more deliberate, the supernatural world sinks farther away.

WILLIAM BUTLER YEATS

The Story: Raised by Wolves

We call it The Back, an untouched two acres of land, its privacy guarded by a wall of thick lilac bushes on one side. On the other side are dense rows of trees lined up like soldiers who never move a muscle. When the lilacs bloom, they're full of bees who make it near impossible and terrifying for me to pass. But I do it anyway. I do it almost every day. To get there, I make a sweeping arc, dip into the neighbor's field, and race slightly downhill, dropping into this lush green layer of my secret life, busy with bugs and birds and imaginary horses who I gallop across the field. Sometimes I ride them. Sometimes I become them. The field holds the most relaxed parts of me. This is the space where I can lie down and run my fingers through my own hair or through the wild alfalfa flowers. It's where I roll on the ground and stretch and sniff the soil, where I hum or sing just to hear and feel the vibration of my own throat. It's mine, this uninterrupted space where I'm free to learn the gifts of nature's wildness.

Most days the dogs come with me, and we explore The Back together. I follow them, and they follow their noses and their curiosities. They've shown me how to follow my own nose and how to use my eyes to see details, how to catch a glimpse of something and track it. Annie is an English Setter who cradled me as a baby, held in the curve of her body as I laid on the floor gripping my own bottle, her fur against my face. My single mother resorted to desperate measures of all kinds, even recruiting Annie into co-parenting. I was a baby with her puppies, alongside them in the whelping box. The nascent wiring of my nervous system synced up with their sounds, their smells, and the warmth of litter life. There's a precise weight and presence of a dog's head as it rests on you that I know in my bones. I always have. Tanya is a young Samoyed who is gradually filling in the gaps as Annie ages and slows down. In the winters, Tanya sleeps outside my bedroom window in an expertly dug hole in the snow. I talk to her through the double panes of storm windows and plastic sheeting taped to the walls in a meager attempt to keep the frigid Michigan winter from sneaking through the failing windows. In the warmer months, I learned to take out the screens and coax Tanya into my room. She then perfected the skill of screen removal on her own and could let herself through any window. For a long time, no one knows how she figured it out. No one knows our process or that I'm her teacher. We have secrets.

I walk myself to the bus stop for school. When the mornings are still dark, Tanya stays close. I've told her I need her nearby. With words, but also with my heart. And I'm quite sure she can hear what my heart needs. She leans against my legs while I stand in the awkward huddle of other children waiting for the bus. Her fur is more like a thick pelt, and when she pushes on my shins, I can push back, nearly resting on the warm cushion of her coat. I talk to the other kids, and we throw rocks at mailboxes. We use sticks to draw in the mud or we pretend we're waiting for a spaceship to land. But there's always this part of me straying, pulled somewhere else. I'm drawn into Tanya's attention, her world view, watching birds scratch at the snow or drops of water fall from icicles. It's like there's a song playing in the background of my life, and you have to have dog ears to hear it. But I hear it. Always. Sometimes Tanya follows the bus to school and the principal has to call the house so someone can come pick her up. She's ever-present in the quietest way. Protective. Calm. Concerned.

It's a confusing place where I live during this era of my childhood. The Back makes sense. So do the dogs. But the house and the people in it worry me. Nothing adds up. The house is a maze of hallways, additions, and remodels pieced together with twists and turns. It's as if certain parts of the house can break off and float away at any moment. They call the house The Mushroom Manor, complete with its own colorful mushroom flag. The flag flies at mast even in the worst weather. When I ask why, there's laughter, and the adults glance at each other and smile. When my mom and I moved in, it was a revolving door of divorced guys and their bachelor buddies. For a while, my room had ten twin-sized beds. It reminded me of the boarding school in the Madeline books or the orphanage in the Annie play. On the weekends, I'd go stay with my dad in his fancy apartment, and the room with the ten beds would fill up with children who I barely knew. On Sunday, I'd go back to The Mushroom Manor, and it would just be me in that strange room with ten beds.

When I ask questions, which I do a lot, they say, "This is okay," or "It's good," or "Everything's fine." When I keep asking, they say, "You're too sensitive, Beth. Stop worrying so much." But I'm right there, and I'm wide-eyed, aware, alert. I'm seeing and feeling it all. The drinking and drugging and lying. People not taking care of themselves or each other. It's like they hold up two fingers and say, "This is ten." I grab a hold of some part of myself that is whole and complete, and I begin to guard it. I take *truth* and *trust* and begin breaking away. It's subtle and internal. I'm still there in body but I begin wrapping up my spirit, almost as if the tenderest part of me has run away from home. I stop looking to them for answers.

There's this moment when I'm standing in the darkest hallway of the house. It's in front of the bedroom that will become mine in a year or two. It's a tight spot, full of adults, and I'm squeezed in, but they seem not to notice me. I feel stuck, physically and emotionally. There are loud voices, shouting, a lot of adult bodies moving up and down the hall. I make my way to the wall and run my hands along textured wallpaper. My nails catch the ridges, and it feels like it's slowing me down. I wait and watch and try to understand. There's a broken-down humidifier gurgling next to me. I'm listening to the adults' words but they're all running together and soaked in emotions and confusing inflections. I can't tell if people are shouting or laughing, if they are enjoying the interaction or about to hurt each other. Behind me, the dogs are standing there. I can feel their noses push on my legs. Their breath is wet, and the rhythm of their panting is a ceremonial drum I can feel in my sternum. I tell myself to pay attention: *Watch this, Beth.* I want to remember. I tell myself: *This is important.* It's like I can carve this memory into the tree trunk of my childhood, and I'll go back and find it later. This is a choice point, my choice point. I lean into the dogs and slowly back my way down the hall, into a darkness that I can live with. The sounds of the human voices fade out. And that feels right.

I guard the girl who knows what she needs. I keep her close to books and dogs. I take her to The Back so she can watch clouds or hear grass soaking up the rain. It's hard to be in the world and take care of her. She doesn't like tights and stiff shoes. She's not a fan of sitting. I mean, she can do it for a while. But the hard plastic chairs at school are like torture. Inherently, she wants to learn and to please and to do well. She wants skills. She gets excellent grades. But social pressures will increase, running on the playground will decrease, and teachers will seem to care less than they used to about her emotional needs. She can sniff out lies and insincerity, and more and more, the human world seems full of that. Pressure to achieve and succeed takes the place of being in the moment, noticing things. As her body changes and matures, she will struggle to find her way into the reverie of glowing fields and dog fur, the imaginative space of an afternoon meandering in textures and movements. She can't find her way back. She will begin to live in her thoughts. Thoughts of self, fears, obsessions about the past or the future. When she's taught to put her hand out and make eye contact, she learns and obliges, but her wholeness will take a hit. She often feels like she's dying inside, a life force dimming. The answer, it seems, is to continue backing away, going inside, into a dangerous desire to be in another world. She wants to run away. But she doesn't know where to go or how to be. She will become a master of disappearance with a handful of unerring tricks that allow her to reside in between worlds. Somewhere between the human world and the animal world is a kind of purgatory. She stays suspended in it, fossilized it seems.

The idea comes like an emotional meteorite. Instead of mass destruction, its impact is an exquisite opening, the first notes of a song I had forgotten I love. *I need a dog. I'm twenty years old. I need a dog now.* No one thinks this is a good idea. They say I can barely take care of myself. They say I need to focus on college. They say people can't have dogs until they've settled down. Not one word of that rings true. Not one. Besides, I had stopped listening to them long ago. I was raised by wolves, those childhood dog companions. They were the stewards of my true self, and I know they would approve. There is no brake system for my plan. Before long, I've met my heart-dog, Levi, who will become my most significant partner as I stumble and falter through a decade of early adulthood.

There's another big moment a few months after Levi came into my world. I'm standing on the edge of two or so acres of rocks and dust, about the same size as The Back. Angora goats nibble on pieces of hay hanging on the wire fence. I tuck my hands in my jean's pockets and I squint past the Arizona sun to watch the goats meander and mull about. Levi is at my side, and I can feel his whole body trembling. It's windy, and sections of tumbleweed scatter past our legs. We both know something significant is about to happen. It's already happening. He's a Border Collie and nearly a year old with a thick puppy muzzle and a flighty eye. He's already so capable and has shown his intelligence in everything we've done. Our connection happened in an instant, two beings fused into partnership as soon as we touched. I've made my way to the outskirts of Phoenix because I'm called to provide for my dog, to fulfill what I learn is his genetic destiny, to give him an opportunity to herd livestock. I've had no exposure to herding, but knowing he has a biological roadmap for it excites me like nothing I've felt in years. I tremble with him as we stand there and track the wooly bodies.

Dodie is the old rancher who has invited us into her world. She's as thin as a goat leg and carries a crook, her minute fingers resting on the polished ram horn handle. She's kind and seems humored by me and Levi as we stand there vibrating with an energy neither of us have ever known. "We'll put him on those goats in a minute. Let me get them settled with my dog." We watch as she and her smooth-coated dog move together. She whistles and this dog turns on a dime, his eyes laser-focused on the goats. *He's moving them with his eye.* His feet barely touch the ground as he slinks about. *It's like he's hunting—but with total control of his own impulses.* Dodie watches him, gives a couple more whistles, and he circles, slows, turns, and then sharply drops to the desert ground. As his chest hits the dirt, I feel my own body drop, a downshift into a new gear; something guttural and primordial has woken up.

The mammal part of my being is flooded with sensation. It's like my blood and bone marrow are on fire. Levi feels this too as we are invited to walk toward Dodie and the goats. "Drop the leash," she says with conviction. I can't. I can't seem to uncurl my fingers from the leather. "Just let it go," she says. Those words reverberate and echo through my brain like an old church bell. The moment slows down. Letting go of the leash seems to take minutes instead of seconds. Memories of The Back come into focus, my pristine freedom and peace with my dogs, the safety and clarity and aliveness I could find with them but had lost with those of my own species. I'm standing in this dusty corral finally reacquainted with the wisest and most intact part of myself. As the leather lead slips out of my hand, I watch my dog ignite into his truest form, body lowered and energy intensified as he slinks around the small grouping of goats. He shifts from dog into wolf. He knows how to move and where to look and when to slow. It only takes a few passes, watching him, feeling him, and I can predict the rhythm of it. Our energy and movement sync up. No words. No commands. No whistles. This earliest experience of herding is raw and untouched.

He lifts the goats from where they have paused, pivots his body to turn them, and using his eye and intention, moves them in my direction. *He's bringing them to me.* It takes my breath away. *He's bringing them to me.* He knows when he feels a balance point, that exact moment and angle to stop. He drops to his belly like Dodie's dog and doesn't take his eyes off the goats. They slow and settle at my feet, an ancient configuration of human, livestock, and dog. The leash is only a memory in my hand, that object of restraint and control. What has emerged is instinct and partnership, consecrated, intact, and wholly accessible. It's right there like it never left, potent and persistent within me, within my dog, within the goat herd. It runs between us, this mammal vitality, an invisible circulatory system bringing blood flow to all of the places where I have been mostly numb. I stand there with this beautiful dog before me, his breath an impossible tempo to follow. He is now my partner, and a new purpose and focus has been born between us. It isn't that he brings me back to life. Rather, he brings my life back to me. And from here, I can go forward and figure out how to live.

The Concept: We Are Human Animals

> Human beings are the only animals who are happily lied to by our own minds about what is actually happening around us.
> **CESAR MILAN**

Human beings are animals. We are sometimes monsters, sometimes magnificent, but always animals. We may prefer to think of ourselves as fallen angels, but in reality we are risen apes.

DESMOND MORRIS

To think of ourselves as mammals, or human animals, is not that far-fetched if you pause long enough to consider your basic knowledge of biology and the animal kingdom. We all know what constitutes a mammal and that humans are situated on the food chain just like every other living thing. Yet, most people recoil at the idea of ourselves as animals. People of all cultures have been moving away from our connection to our mammalian roots for thousands of years. It seems the more sophisticated our capacities become for rational thought, innovation, industry, and creative expression, the less we have remained consistently connected to the primitive parts of us that signal our fundamental needs. The more lost and busy in thought, language, relationship, and daily trans-actions, the less we can access or attend to ourselves in the simple and honest ways that our basic organism needs. Desmond Morris, in his book, *The Human Animal*, explores our species from the unique perspective of a zoologist, reminding us, "We owe far more to our animal inheritance than we are usually prepared to admit. But instead of being ashamed of our animal nature, we can view it with respect. If we understand it and accept it, we can actually make it work for us." With our robust rational brain dominating, we live without nearly enough access to the wealth of messages and inner resources that are designed to guide us to care for our-selves and others. These include our natural instincts, drives, body signals, and wise survival practices. Sound ancient and mystical? Well, they aren't! These are powerful and practical tools for living and relating, and they are at the heart of how we stabilize ourselves as individuals and make the cultures and relationship norms safer in our groups, families, teams, and communities. Recovering this aspect of our innate capacities as mammals is how humans can connect with and begin to use our Natural Leadership.

So how did we become what Morris refers to as "this compulsively curious, constantly chattering creature" who moves about the world with fundamental blind spots in our survival system? How did we lose touch with this mammalian part of us that is so crucial in interpreting our needs and the needs of others? And how do we reignite our human animal so that we can integrate its signal system and enhance the functioning of this magnificent modern brain? It turns out that as the human brain evolved over time, it developed a bit of a glitch. To understand it better, it helps to have a basic understanding of the brains and how we differ from other mammals.

The Power of Understanding Our Brains

Emerging research and technologies in the last thirty years have helped us to understand our brains in a much more comprehensive way and this allows us to become strategic and empowered in a process of working with the brains we have. I had a front-row seat to this new perspective as a psychotherapist in training during the time when cognitive neuroscience came on the scene and began to shed this new and crucial light on human brain functioning. Since the 1990s, positron emission tomography (PET) and functional magnetic resonance imaging (fMRI) have been used to provide real-time brain imaging, showing how blood flows in different regions of the brain during our whole range of mental activities. With this technology, we can see which parts of our brain are recruited and which parts are abandoned during a variety of circumstances. This allows us to understand how our complex emotional and survival system impacts our daily experiences. We can also see how our capacities to cope are influenced by the different regions of the brain. The work of eminent psychiatrist, Daniel Siegel, has been instrumental in bringing the field of neuroscience first into the field of counseling and therapy and then into the mainstream. Siegel writes, "In a brain scan, relational pain—that is caused by isolation during punishment—can look the same as physical abuse." While we don't need to take a deep dive into neuroscience, it makes good sense to use the knowledge of the brain we now have so we can be engaged with our biology, be informed about how we operate, and become strategic about how we move through the stressors of life.

Brain Basics

In the 1960s, neuroscientist Paul MacLean described the regions of the human brain in his triune brain theory. This evolutionary view of brain development divides the brain into three distinct and integral areas based on hierarchy of needs. It's almost as if the human brain is composed of three interconnected brains: a reptile brain, a mammal brain, and a thinking brain. Dan Siegel's work has been responsible for bringing the triune brain into conversation for the past twenty years. I had the pleasure and honor of attending several of his workshops early in my career as a therapist, and the training profoundly changed my professional work. Just as important, it deeply impacted my personal development. I began to realize how my early experiences with dogs and horses shaped me, and it began to crystalize why I had continued to gravitate to animals into my adulthood.

As I learned about my own triune brain, my relationship to myself, other humans, my animals, and the world around me, it inspired me to use my brain more actively and to become more aware of the interplay between my emotions and my thoughts. It occurred to me along the way that I had been asking my dogs and horses to cope with situations that triggered their survival centers. And they could do it! With partnership, support, and the opportunity to be curious and to learn, all of my animals developed an emotional resilience that prepared them to calmly move through an unpredictable world. If they could do it, so could I. So could most other humans. I became more intentional and adept at detecting when my own brain regions were active and working with the ebbs and flows of emotional reactivity. It's a lot like learning to use the core muscles of your abdomen. At first, you can't even figure out how to trigger the muscles to fire. But as you practice, you can target muscle groups by focusing your mind, and before you know it, the communication with those muscles is seamless, which makes them more usable. Siegel writes about this, "One of the key practical lessons of modern neuroscience is that the power to direct our attention has within it the power to shape our brain's firing patterns, as well as the power to shape the architecture of the brain itself."

To start, we need a basic understanding of the brain regions. The primitive brain region is a lot like a reptile and is responsible for our basic survival functions like breathing, body temperature, and our startle response. The mammalian, or the emotional brain, is the reactive part of us that feels threat and responds with fight, flight, or freeze. This is also the part of our brain that drives our empathy system, cares for our young, and has the capacity to notice and attend to needs in others and in our groups. The neocortex is our thinking brain, responsible for our problem-solving, reasoning, and all conscious activity such as language, abstract cognition, creativity, and planning. This beautiful "meaning maker" creates art and literature, constructs narratives about our lives and our identities, and pursues innovation. This is the part of our brain that makes us uniquely human and separates us from the rest of the animal world.

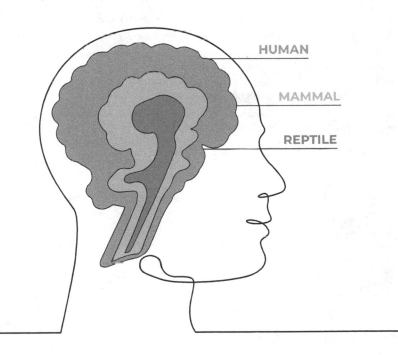

THE ANCIENT REPTILIAN BRAIN	• Vital control centers; brainstem; primitive functioning • Startle response; totally reactive • No emotional life; no relationship with young; indifference to others
MAMMALS: THE LIMBIC BRAIN/ SYSTEM	• Mediates emotions like fear, anger, and sadness • Stores information as "implicit memory" • Regulates brainstem and coordinates internal states with environmental states • Interest in the social world; social world impacts how we regulate our bodies • Coordinates internal world of oneself with internal world of others • Orientation toward offspring; mother/infant bonding but no intimacy
THE NEOCORTEX	• Enables us to reflect on abstract ideas and think about the future • Capacity for language • Capacity for self-reflection and making meaning of events in our lives • Integrates emotional and physical experience

The Human Brain Glitch

But here's the catch. The human animal can continue talking, thinking, and relating even when the neocortex is not getting adequate blood flow. In short, our brains get hijacked into a full-blown fear response without our knowledge of it. We talk or think our way through these reactive storms. And we believe all of the thoughts our brain is creating even though they may not be based in reality. We can think or talk ourselves into all kinds of bad assumptions, behaviors, and choices. When this glitch occurs, which it does often, we are disconnected from the signals our bodies are sending, and therefore we do not adjust or take care of our needs. Our body is experiencing a four-alarm fire, and our brain just keeps making thoughts and our mouth just keeps making words.

In its extremes, this brain glitch is at the root of psychological disorders such as PTSD. Peter Levine's book, *Waking the Tiger*, describes this phenomenon with great clarity, "When confronted with a life-threatening situation, our rational brains may become confused and override our instinctive impulses." When this happens, our bodies are flooded with mobilizing survival chemicals and our thoughts are telling us something contradictory. The impact of those chemicals is corrosive and interrupts a natural process of the mammal fight, flight, or freeze response. Though many of our daily occurrences don't constitute traumas, we must consider the impact of a human thought process that overrides our instincts to attend to needs in the face of daily pressure and stress. When a horse feels pressure, it notices and responds. When a human feels pressure, we keep thinking and talking, and we try to our hardest to ignore it.

The more that we learn the signals of the mammalian brain and how it feels in our bodies when our survival system mobilizes, the more efficient we can become at making slight adjustments and meeting our own needs. So much of the work of Natural Leadership is about sensing the mammal within and listening and attending to what is being communicated.

Oversocialization of the Human Animal

We don't come into the world with a fog blocking access to our primitive signal system. In fact, our development tracks the same development as a chimpanzee for the first twenty-one months of life, until the language centers of the human brain come online, and we begin our diversion from our primate friends. Pediatrician Harvey Karp helps us understand that between one and four years old, a child's "rapid maturation will greatly resemble a superfast rerun of ancient human development . . . the same great achievements that took our primitive ancestors eons to master spring forth in our children over the space of just three years." During those months of life, human babies and toddlers are entirely committed to their impulses, drives, sensations, and needs. On the one hand, we certainly all benefit from control over hitting, biting, or throwing food and feces like our primate relatives. However, in our efforts to socialize our young, we are teaching them to suppress needs and to ignore their bodies.

Freud wrote, "It is impossible to overlook the extent to which civilization is built upon a renunciation of instinct." In so many of our global cultures, civilized life, and the social codes we follow as good villagers, teach us to suppress the body's impulses. We can see a lot of this in typical classrooms. When my daughter started kindergarten in a fairly traditional school, she cried for a week because she had to sit at a desk and could no longer learn on the floor. Her teacher, who had decades of experience teaching in the Montessori philosophy, told me that each kindergartener fell out of the chairs at least one time per day. So why were they sitting in chairs? How did we decide small children needed to sit at desks? Maria Montessori wrote about this, saying, "The child, like every strong creature fighting for the right to live, rebels against whatever offends that occult impulse within him which is the voice of nature, and which he ought to obey." So much of the disruptive behavior that occurs in school-age children comes from a cycle of needs suppression. We ask our children to sit, to be quiet, to be indoors, and to focus for far longer than they are developmentally able. Of course, we see signs and symptoms. The younger the child, the more immediate and honest the feedback about what is off-balance and what it is they need.

Children and animals offer the adult human animal a very important window into the world of basic needs, radical honesty, and self-preservation. How many times have you seen animals and children gravitate to each other and the immediacy of trust that occurs? The attraction between them is based on an authenticity and presence that is linked to our needs system. Maria Montessori understood that our learning motivation comes from our mammal instincts to develop and survive. "The rewards which the child reaps also remain between him and nature," she writes. "The child as a rule has for his unconscious desire, his own self-development." Her prescribed model of learning honored the balance of learning social structures and civilized life while maintaining a life force fully connected to our inner nature. "It is true that man has created enjoyments in social life and has brought about a vigorous human love in community life. But nevertheless, he still belongs to nature, and, especially when he is a child, he must draw from it the forces necessary to the development of the body and of the spirit. We have intimate communications with nature which have an influence, even a material influence, on the growth of the body," wrote Montessori. These same principles apply to every living human, regardless of age. Yet, in so much of our Western culture, we have conceded to a way of life that ignores the needs of our animal selves. The rigid elementary school desk becomes a sterile work cubicle.

Implications and Consequences for a Neglected Human Animal

What is it like for a human animal to exist in many of the cultural paradigms in which we live? The pressure to fit into social norms can overemphasize polish and poise to a dangerous degree. We walk through our contemporary lives, lost in our intellectual world, our nervous systems flooded in overstimulated environments. Our cities are crowded, our schedules are overbooked, our workplaces are stifling. These unforgiving elements take a toll, and our inner animal retreats in order to protect itself. We are either too numb or busy to notice the messages from our inner world, so our instincts are left ignored and our needs unattended to.

With this primary part of ourselves missing or impaired, our physical health suffers. As individuals, our mental wellness limps along, so we can't show up fully with others. Our sense of community is fractured. Without attention to this part of us, we are not able to take proper care of ourselves and also are not as equipped to sense what is happening with those around us. Because the human organism is incredibly resilient and can bear tremendous stress, it can take years or decades before we notice the symptoms that our health has been compromised and our mental and physical health—even our survival—is at risk. Jeffrey Pfeffer, in his groundbreaking book, *Dying for a Paycheck*, looks at the corporate epidemic of workplace stress: "Companies have developed elaborate measures to track their progress on environmental sustainability with little thought given to the companies' effects on *human* sustainability."

We need only glance at the data to see the increasing numbers of mental illnesses, psychiatric diagnoses in children, and work-related stress injuries. There are, of course, other critical factors in our family, work, and community systems that affect our health and functioning. But by getting to know this basic part of ourselves, the human animal body, we have the power to effect immediate change. From there, we may very well be inspired to help, lead, or teach, but our calls to service and productivity have a better chance of success and sustainability if we are engaged in radical self-care. To use a phrase from the world of addiction and codependency recovery: *Let it begin with me.*

We Have Needs

It seems an obvious statement. We have needs. Of course we have needs! But think about it—how well-versed are you with your own needs? How often do you tune inward to identify where you can rebalance or adjust? Do you live with an underlying belief that self-care comes second or last—or never? Consider for a moment how many times your body told you that you need to use the restroom and you decided to wait. Or how many times you have felt thirsty and postponed the drink of water for hours. What about when a person is talking too loud or too fast and your body tightens? There are dozens of times per day when we ignore the signals of the body and our physical, emotional, and social needs are left in a lurch. Often I imagine what the animals would say if we told them how many of our needs we ignore. Perhaps they already know. It's why they ask us to walk and play, why they slow us down and show us interesting things, why they drop their heads and cue us to breathe, why they request or even insist that we get on the ground and hug them. They feel us deeply, and they do what they can to communicate and illuminate the truth about our needs.

We don't usually become acquainted with our needs until we feel pressure in its extremes. We hit a point of exhaustion or overwhelm, like an internal rock bottom. Other times, we come into intense conflict in relationships because we have been overextending with others or not asking for help. Worse yet, our bodies will show symptoms of stress, or our mental health will deteriorate and that's when we wake up and pay attention to ourselves. Our thoughts, feelings, sensations, and behaviors give us clues and signs about what is off-kilter or out of balance. Yet we ignore those subtle cues, telling ourselves that attending to our needs is optional and can wait. Many of us live on autopilot because we have been socialized, or oversocialized, to muscle forward, carry on, and persevere as if those qualities are badges of honor. The culture of our families and workplaces overvalue self-sufficiency. We critique neediness and view it as a weakness. We have all kinds of conscious and unconscious beliefs about our needs that affect how we lead ourselves and ultimately how we lead or relate with others.

COMMON MISCONCEPTIONS ABOUT SELF CARE	REALITIES ABOUT SELF CARE
Self care is all about bubble baths, massages, and reading good books.	Self care is a daily practice of adjusting to your internal and external pressures so you can live in balance.
If you take time for your own needs, you are being selfish or self indulgent.	In order to maintain your stability, you do need to focus on yourself first and foremost. You're also able to be aware and care about others' needs.
Committing to your needs means you are neglecting others.	Self care IS care for others. When you take good care of yourself, you are able to show up with the best parts of yourself and be better able to support others.
Others will judge you if you have healthy boundaries or take time for yourself.	People are often confused when you shift your approach to self care. Yet, you will find others feel inspired and want more self care for themselves.

But here's the truth about needs: We have hundreds of needs all day, every day. It's just a fact of life. The good news is that our instincts to survive are alive and well. We do end up taking care of some of our needs without even realizing it. When we become more aware and intentional about our needs, we can improve how we function, minimize our stressors, conserve energy, get more support from others, and feel more at ease and fulfilled. We can reclaim our power.

Become a Student of Your Animal Body Signals

To begin this reclamation project, we want to broaden our awareness of the signals our human animal body offers. We're used to listening to signals from our rational mind because of the sheer magnitude of thoughts our brain automatically creates. According to a 2020 study from Queens University in Canada by Julie Tseng and Jordan Poppenk, humans have approximately 6,200 thoughts per day. It is an incredibly dominant part of the human animal experience, a loud static that diminishes the quality of the mammal notes we ought to hear.

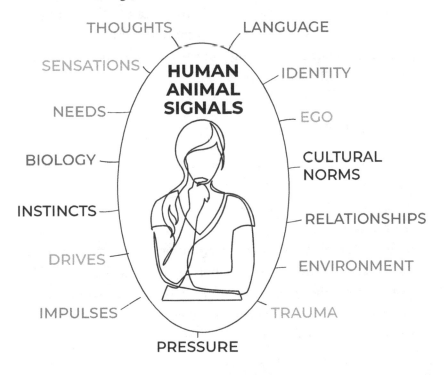

THOUGHTS   LANGUAGE

SENSATIONS

HUMAN ANIMAL SIGNALS

IDENTITY

NEEDS

EGO

BIOLOGY

CULTURAL NORMS

INSTINCTS

RELATIONSHIPS

DRIVES

ENVIRONMENT

IMPULSES

TRAUMA

PRESSURE

Your Mammal Awareness in Action

You'll find that as you tune in to your mammalian signals, it's shockingly simple to reconnect. That's the beauty of Natural Leadership. We already possess it. Our hardwiring to survive and thrive is fully intact, and with awareness and practice, we are able to gain quite a bit of usable access. Basically, you mobilize your emotional, relational, intellectual, and mammal intelligence, and in so doing, you and those around you will notice a big shift. This wordless language sends signals to others that you are stable. Because you are! There is a sequence to this. Your attention to needs allows you to care for yourself. Your self-care creates internal stability in your whole being. When you are grounded and stable, those around you can feel it and are drawn to it. The rule of thumb is that mammal nervous systems will always sync up with the most stable nervous system in proximity. Imagine, for a moment, the implications here. Our self-care is at the root of our leadership and partnership with others. Regardless of our relational role, hierarchy, or setting, our self-leadership and the care for our mammalian self is everything.

How to Care for Your Mammal Self

The first and perhaps most important step is to carve out a mindset or inquiry about our own needs as human animals. In essence, we have to become students of ourselves. We are quite similar in terms of our basic needs; however, each one of us has a unique "secret sauce" or formula for our hourly, daily, and weekly lives that allows us to find our balance points. The more you learn about yourself, the easier it is to get into a practice and routine around your needs that becomes second nature. Here's a daily inventory you can use to become an ally to your own needs.

BODY
physical nourishment and care

WORK
purposeful contributions

EMOTIONS
support and soothing

MIND
intellectual learning

WHAT AM I NEEDING?

CREATIVITY
novel ideas and imagination

SPIRITUAL
service to the greater good

RELATIONSHIPS
connection

The Practice: Take Your Animal Body for a Walk

WARNING: *You're going to read this exercise and balk at it! You might think some of these thoughts: "No way. Not me. That's too long of a time to do this exercise. I'm not going to like this. I'm going to get bored." It's okay. You are not alone! Many before you have felt the same when faced with this exercise. Go with it. The doubt and unease are normal and absolutely part of the process. Freedom is on the other side.*

1. You will spend twenty minutes alone and in silence. Use your phone so that you can set a timer but refrain from checking it while you're doing this exercise.

2. You're going to take a walkabout. This is much different than a purposeful walk with a destination or a goal in mind. This is a meander, a wander, an exploration. You will allow your body—your beautiful and wise human animal body—to go where it wants to go and to do what it wants to do.

3. Follow your curiosity and see where it takes you. You are likely going to notice things around you. When something catches your attention, go with it. Let it lead you. Stay with the things you notice as long as you want. Really study and explore the things that catch your eye or ear or nose. Let your senses guide you.

4. You may find that you want to sit or lie down during the walkabout. Go for it! You may want to walk fast or walk slow. Go with that! If you are inclined to sit, give it a try. If you discover that it isn't working for you and you want to walk again, then give yourself permission to get up and walk. You might find yourself struggling to know what to do with yourself. This is normal. Your body is trying to settle in and get its needs met. Our minds are very busy overriding our bodies' needs all day long. This twenty minutes will allow your body to be in charge. Experiment and let your body tell you what it desires and needs.

One of the best ways to get to know your mammal self is to begin to ask it questions. It will feel awkward at first, and you may even experience a sensation of shyness. This is because you are getting to know a part of yourself that is inherently sensitive, introverted, and shy. The mammal part of you is slow to warm to strangers and won't always trust the thinking part of you to lead. Here are a few questions to get you started in a dialogue with your mammal self:

- When you slowed down and gave yourself permission to be curious and to wander, what caught your attention? What brought you awe?
- What was the ONE thing that most resonated and touched your spirit?
- What thoughts did you have that interrupted your curiosity or your ability to be present? What thoughts helped you to be more curious?
- What emotions did you have as you wandered? How did your heart feel?
- If you think about your daily life, what is the impact of not having enough time and space for you to "settle in?" How has that hurt you?
- If you consider the natural rhythm of your weekdays or your weekends, what are some obvious times when it would help you to settle in or to transition from one activity to the next? How can you plan for this and commit to it?
- If you bring your human animal instincts to your relationships, how might you engage with others differently? How might this new awareness of your mammal-self impact how you show up in your marriage, in your work setting, or with your parenting?

CHAPTER TWO

Awareness

If the sure animal that approaches us
in a different direction had this awareness of ours,
he would drag us along behind him. But his existence
is infinite to him, ungrasped, without a glimpse
at his condition, pure as his outward gaze.
And where we see the future, he sees All
and himself in All and himself healed forever.

RANIER MARIA RILKE

There is always something new to notice.

ELLEN LANGER

The Story: Waking Up

We walked along the barn aisles as eager faces reached toward us asking for connection, ears pricked forward and nostrils flaring to catch a whiff of hormones, a trace of our story. We were looking for a red roan filly we were there to meet, but we passed dozens of horse stalls and hadn't come across her yet. When I decided to look for a new horse, I had an instinctive call, a barely conscious curiosity about wanting a mare. In my childhood years, I had enjoyed the friendship of female dogs and horses, but the animals of my adulthood had all been male. In the horse world, mares get a bad rap. A lot of people say that they're difficult, moody, opinionated, and not worth the headache of a more mercurial relationship. "Mare-ish" is a word you'll hear, and you'll see a lot of eyes roll when people describe them. Something about this always caught my attention. It sounded discriminatory and a bit extreme, similar to what people say about teenagers—and women. It rubbed me the wrong way, but it affected me and likely impacted my choices for male animals along the way.

Still, I had this inner longing for a mare. I'd found some very nice horses in my search, but each time I met a new one, something fell flat. There was this missing piece, and I struggled to name it. We came around the corner of the barn and entered a busy area where several horses stood tied to hitching posts. The crooning baritone of a country singer floated out of dusty lo-fi speakers. Pigeons cooed from the rafters where thin slices of daylight glowed, polishing each bird like silver. I quickly scanned the horses, and my attention stuck as soon as I saw the filly. I caught her eye in my line of sight, and she caught mine. We locked into place, a perfect fit, an alignment I could feel in my skin. I still couldn't articulate it, but the red roan filly had that certain spark I had been awaiting.

I went through the formalities of meeting her and riding her. I asked questions and looked her over carefully. I noticed her asymmetries and imperfections as much as I noticed her beauty and talent. None of it mattered. From that very first moment of feeling her presence, I had already decided she was my horse. "You know when you know," I told my friend Tami who accompanied me that day. Tami smiled and seemed to understand. After a lifetime of bonding with her own equine partners, Tami got it on the deepest level. "You know when you know," she answered back.

We drove back to my house where Tami had left her truck, chatting about the filly and all things horse. Our friendship was still new, but we had horses in common, and there was something settled and grounding about Tami that drew me to her. We sat in my driveway for a bit, and I felt myself linger. I don't know what compelled me to say it, but the conversation I started with Tami that day may have saved my life. "I stopped drinking a few weeks ago," I told her. She nodded and listened. No pressure. No questions. No judgment. Perhaps it was her years of sobriety that helped her to know how fragile and tenuous I was in that moment. "I've been so anxious. I can barely stand being in my own skin." Still, she just listened. Waited. It was quiet. The pauses hung like ripe fruit.

"Do you know why you stopped drinking?" Tami asked. I spun out with the question, frantic with fits and starts of sentences I couldn't figure out how to finish. I talked myself into a corner and then I stopped. I just stopped uttering words. It was quiet again. Then she asked the bravest question anyone had ever asked me, "Do you think you're an alcoholic?"

It had been a slow but steady unraveling, like a knit sweater coming apart and losing its shape one stitch at a time. But I had been coming undone for years. There was a gradual dimming, the most alive parts of me fading. It didn't start out that way. No, I was always a "noticer of things," sensitive and picking up on subtleties and nuances. When I was just three years old, I went with my mom to a meeting in a newspaper editor's office, every inch of the walls plastered with photos and news clippings. I stood there for a few moments scanning the images until I pointed and exclaimed, "Look Mommy! It's Jimmy Tarter!"

With incredible attention to detail and a tightly wound empathy system, my sensitivity was like a superpower. But it was also my kryptonite. It allowed me to linger and feel the beauty and awe of life, but it also meant that I felt difficult emotions with intensity as well. I had no idea how to live with the pressures and stressors and unknowns. I was wide awake to the abscesses in the humanity around me. Up and down the hallways of my life, and much of it rooted in childhood, there was so much confusion and pain: parents walking away from relationships, lost adults, neglected children, abuse, self-destruction, anti-Semitism, the cruelty of other children. The world around me and within me felt profoundly unsafe and certainly not kind to the sensitivity within me. Perhaps the hardest truth was that I had no idea how to cope.

I picked up my first drink when I was twelve years old. I don't really know why. But I do know what the drinking did. It gave me a tough persona, a costume to wear so I could pretend to be someone who wasn't terrified of just about everything. It changed the way I felt inside, smoothed out my awkward and lonely edges. It allowed me to not care about the mess of paradoxes that couldn't be resolved. I didn't want to die, but I didn't know how to live. I didn't want to be seen, but I didn't want to be forgotten. I wanted to find answers, meaning, and clarity, but I desperately needed to lose my mind, to orbit in a dizzying constellation of noise, chaos, and relief. But when I picked up that first drink on that first night and had that first sensation, it was as if a gear shifted into place. I found a space inside of myself where I could finally breathe. It was numbness. I chased numbness for a long time. We chased each other. I was the ouroboros spinning in circles and devouring myself in a cycle of being lost and trying to get unlost.

Spiritual awakenings are those times when our awareness of ourselves and how we fit into the bigger picture of our lives come into very clear focus. They're like turnstiles. The opening occurs for an instant. Like a camera flash that lights the darkness. There's a window during which you have the capacity to question your choices, who you have become, and who you want to be. In those brief flashes of *holy crap*, your morality is right there with you, a solid definition of what matters most to you, a sense of right and wrong. It's your higher self, your best self, your goodness. It's looking at you in the mirror and holding you accountable. Then the moment is gone.

My final drunk escapade was a boring, run-of-the-mill bar-beque complete with a full-blown blackout. Emails the next day indicated that I'd seemed to have had intelligent conversations, been charming, proposed some lunch plans and professional collaborations, and even arranged to share a ride to some random musical event I had no intention of attending. The first real memories came into focus as I curled up around the toilet, nauseous and horrified. I was there again, empty and sick inside, a mind swirling with remorse and fear. *How did this happen? How did I do this to myself? Again.*

Then it struck me to my core: *How are you going to become a parent if you keep doing this?* In that painful gray area of dawn when I dangled in a crevasse of awareness, the sharpness of that question woke me up like a shard of ice crashing between my eyes. I knew everything in that moment. There was a bigger life asking me to show up. The question surprised me because I didn't even know if I wanted to become a mom. I didn't know what I wanted to become. That was the problem. I just wasn't moving forward of my own volition. I rested my head on the coolness of the toilet seat, desperate to pass out and stop feeling the rotten interior of that morning. I may have said it out loud. *It's time to wake up.*

Our journey began that day when the red roan filly named Rosie's gaze locked with mine and I saw that she had the open channel of alertness and connection I needed. Unbeknownst to me, I was asking for a certain kind of guide. Almost instantly, Rosie became that for me, my teacher and partner back to the world of sensitivity and awareness. The conversation with Tami in my driveway stayed with me. It stayed and it festered until I was more ready and more miserable. As they often do, the parallel narratives in our lives eventually converge. We don't know our stories are headed to a meeting place until they get there. But once they do, everything makes sense.

I started to ride Rosie and get to know her inner world as I began to feel my own. It helped that I was staying sober and learning my interior landscape through the structures and support of recovery. I was learning to wake up and stay awake, to listen to her awareness and to hear my own. Rosie was carrying my sensitivity, and I was learning to carry hers. This kind of partnership was new to me, even after a lifetime with horses. There's quite a lot she needed in order for me to be a solid partner for her. I had never known such a responsive horse, an animal who could read my mind, feel the slightest shift in my energy, and predict my next move. It was almost like I had to learn to ride all over again. Rosie's desire to partner with me and her exquisite vitality prepared me for my daughter who would later enter the world with a similar makeup, an intuitive soul who doesn't miss a thing. When Emma was born, more pieces of my story and Rosie's role in it came into focus.

Eventually, I was able to give Rosie the gift of pasture freedom and a herd. My horse herd expanded, and Rosie's most unique gift of awareness became more apparent in the context of horse culture. Sometimes referred to as The Queen of Awareness, Rosie has always been the first to notice anything new or changed in the environment. If a leaf falls from a tree, Rosie knows. If the cows are coming over the hill, she will stand waiting and watching for ten to fifteen minutes before they are even visible. If I open the door to the house and walk toward the barn, she alerts the herd to mobilize and meet me. Her role comes with a cost and must be balanced and supported by other herd members. Without feedback and signals from the others, her sensitivity can look and feel hypervigilant and nervous. The herd, just by way of staying in a state of ease and homeostasis, reminds her when it's safe to relax and let go by sharing awareness so that she can pass the baton of her role. She has also learned to care for her heightened awareness. She positions herself on the perimeter of the herd so she can cover more ground at a faster pace. Moving her body allows that vibrant awareness energy to be used and to pass through her so that she isn't ridden with anxiety.

I've studied and joined Rosie's awareness journey from the saddle and the field, on her back and walking alongside her. For many years we've traveled and covered thousands of miles, explored hills and trails, beaches and rivers, new places and old. We've stood quietly together and noticed things. The more I've relaxed into my own awareness gifts, the better I've cared for myself and set up a life and daily flow that allows me to stay in awareness without harm. As Rosie has matured, she's settled into her awareness. When we met, we were like live wires, sparking and reactive to a world that didn't support sensitivity as a gift. We breathe deeper now, can take longer and slower steps. We pause and consider. We look to our herd members for support. We know how to use our awareness, how to protect it, and how to rest it.

The Concept: Awareness Is a Superpower

Awareness is a natural capacity for all mammals. All mammals, humans included, have an innate ability to utilize multiple channels of awareness in order to attend to our own needs, to sense the internal state of those around us, to navigate relationships, and to notice and respond to changes and pressures in our surroundings. Being aware on this level is key to our individual and group survival. When we turn to nature and the animals, Natural Leadership Awareness can become easier to grasp and to see practiced and lived. Though our animal friends do not operate with a metacognition or consciousness that we know of, their Natural Leadership Awareness is always present and fully alive. Without the burden of a thinking brain or language to disrupt the natural frequencies of awareness, animals very much live in the moment and take in all of the signals within and around them. Their survival depends on an alertness and a radical commitment to attending to needs. The human herd relies on this as well, though unless it is learned and cultivated, our human version of Natural Leadership Awareness exists in a much narrower space, one that limits our commitment to caring for ourselves and others.

When we work with the concept of Natural Leadership Awareness, we must not fall prey to the typical human habit of focusing only on our thoughts, a trap to which we are especially prone. Even though mindfulness, by definition, encompasses more than attunement to our thinking brain, it is often associated with meditation and/or the practice of working with our thoughts. Awareness and mindfulness are often used synonymously. To avoid setting our language on autopilot, we must instead slow down and be intentional about how we talk about this. We can take a cue from psychologist Ellen Langer, the "mother of mindfulness." When she began to use the word, she did so in order to describe the counterpoint to mindlessness. "Mindlessness is pervasive," she writes. "In fact I believe virtually all of our problems—personal, interpersonal, professional, and societal—either directly or indirectly stem from mindlessness."

The Thinking Problem

The mind is a thought generator and can be considered to be the brain's "exhaust system." Of our 6,200 thoughts per day, cognitive research indicates that 80 percent are negative and 95 percent are repetitive thoughts. Essentially, the human mind is what psychologist David Schnarch referred to as a "meaning making machine." Our brain's neocortex is like a story factory, garnering context and significance from our experiences. We are obsessed with thoughts and have a cultural bias for our cognitive/intellectual functioning. Thinking has prestige. Thinking or "thinking about thinking" causes us to miss cues from other parts of our mammal awareness. It's not that thoughts don't matter or that our executive functioning is altogether negative. It's just that we allow it to be dominant and to drown out the rest of our Natural Leadership capacities that are needed in order to optimize our functioning as mammals.

To put it more bluntly, we are primarily self-absorbed. Humans hyper focus on thoughts to the point of missing crucial information. Coupled with the overreliance on language, thinking becomes a kind of noise of the mind, overshadowing a huge layer of our experience. The way we think about, talk about, and practice mindfulness has a focus on the world of thought. It isn't that a study of thought and mindset is altogether faulty. Rather, our health and functioning rely on a broader scope, providing us with the information we need to function. Ellen Langer writes, "A mindful state also implies openness to new information. Like category making,

the receiving of new information is a basic function of living creatures." An inclusive state of awareness, one that tunes into more
parts of ourselves, others, and other environments, is the basis of
our survival system, the central force by which we lead ourselves
through the world and the necessary function allowing any mammal group to share space and resources and to negotiate needs.

What Is Happening Right Now?

As a very observant and highly sensitive child, my internal
system was often flooded. I noticed things with an often painful
and confusing acuity. I had to learn along the way to use a volume
control on the "noise" and how to cope. Without knowing exactly
what I was up to, I devoted a great deal of my education and professional life as a therapist to finding a solution to the problem
of sensitivity and awareness. In many ways, therapists work with
people to help them learn to cope. I first learned of this awareness
in a more intentional way when I began studying with the forma-
tive mentor of mine, who I mentioned in the introduction, the
late psychologist, Jim Maddock. His teachings live on, especially
in this aspect of my life and work. As a young therapist, it was easy
to get lost in narrative content and the emotions of my clients. I
needed only return to that foundational meta question that had
already changed my life: *What is happening right now?* It lifted me
out of action, relating, or the thought trap and into a new kind of
awareness. It gave me scope and space, the natural element of perspective that allows us to use our higher functioning and to cope.

Over time the question began to feel like pumping the brakes
on a slippery road, a safer way to stop so that the dynamic world
of relationships and living didn't get going faster than I could
process. The question became baked into my being, and I found
myself asking it, especially when I was with my animals. I became

aware that the horse herd, though not consciously using inquiry to function, operated entirely with multiple channels of awareness as a core element of their system. Jim's one question evolved into four questions. Having practiced the use of these with thousands of people, groups, and in hundreds of settings, I've come to understand these awareness questions as the foundation of our survival. Asking these questions and finding the answers allows each of us and all of us to discover our needs. When we know our needs, we can attend to them. This is how we thrive.

THE FOUR QUESTIONS OF NATURAL LEADERSHIP AWARENESS

WHAT IS HAPPENING INSIDE ME?
Powerful leadership begins internally and is directly dependent on our awareness of our emotions, thoughts, physical sensations, and actions.

WHAT IS HAPPENING WITHIN YOU?
Trust and psychological safety require that we seek to understand others, look for similarities that connect us, and see the needs, pain points, and fears of those around us.

WHAT IS HAPPENING BETWEEN US?
In order to create a relationship of trust and resilience, we must shape it through ongoing honest and open feedback.

WHAT IS HAPPENING IN THE ENVIRONMENT?
Our relationships and groups are more secure, prepared, and adaptable if we notice and attend to the factors in our surroundings that affect us all. This is a shared responsibility.

Integrating the Four Channels of Awareness

In Natural Leadership Awareness, we expand our scope in order to gather signals from within, more like our mammal counterparts. We bring the primitive layers of the human animal body to the forefront and ask for information. We give our instinct more voice.

I used to visit my grandparents every couple of months. Their house was frozen in time, furniture covered in plastic to keep it perfect and new, carpet with vacuum lines like the precise lanes of a highway. Winston cigarettes and fresh Danish pastries on the table and always a pot of coffee. A stack of newspapers and a can full of freshly sharpened pencils sat on the counter next to a small transistor radio, which had, somewhere along the way, replaced a police scanner—my grandmother's commitment to awareness had her chasing ambulances and fire trucks until she gave that up. The transistor radio sat next to the kitchen sink and was always tuned to AM news radio, volume low. From anywhere in their house, you could just make out the soothing voices of the broad-casters and the top-of-the-hour musical jingle. It was a constant link to the outside world, and an auditory link to the world inside the house. It was, quite literally, a signal coming into their home, traveling throughout the space and keeping them connected. Our channels of Natural Leadership Awareness are like that transistor radio. Always on. We can turn the volume up or down. We can practice tuning in. We can find a frequency of awareness that allows us to live more intentionally. We can also learn to use the volume control to protect our nervous system so that we can effectively maintain and use our natural sensitivities.

The Benefits of Awareness

Cultivating our awareness capacity allows us to have more self-leadership. When we are conscious of what is happening within and around us, we can respond with choice instead of reaction. The pause of awareness is the precursor to healthy coping. In

NATURAL LEADERSHIP AWARENESS CHANNELS

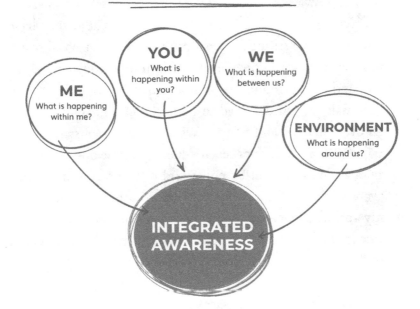

the broader sense, we can see the big picture of our surroundings, which helps us to decide how to orient ourselves in the world. In a more direct and up-close way, awareness allows us to notice the finest details. When we listen to our thoughts, body, instincts, relational feedback, and environmental signals, we get a more honest story about who we are. Knowing ourselves on this level is incredibly empowering and helps us to avoid repeating reactivity patterns that can cause damage to ourselves and our relationships. This kind of emotional freedom provides a new and clear path for us to experience joy and to savor the experiences in our lives. Chade-Meng Tan, a Google engineer who became known as the company's "Jolly Good Fellow" talks about "thin slices of joy." According to Tan, the act of being aware and noticing things allows us to feel the pleasantness of the moment.

Awareness Makes Us Safer

On the most practical level, an integrated and expansive Natural Leadership Awareness is actually a function of safety. When we consider people in our lives with whom we feel safest, they have acute awareness as a strong leadership trait. On the survival front, with more awareness we can attend to our animal body and adjust ourselves and our surroundings so that our nervous system benefits. Mammals are not designed to be in a constant state of stress with an overwhelmed and flooded system. Yet humans are socialized to ignore many of our necessary cues. We stifle our needs, setting them aside in order to be polite and tolerant. A more expansive awareness instead gives us a chance to attend to our needs honestly and wholly. Not only is this safer for us on an individual basis but it also means that we can be more reliable members of our families, friend groups, work teams, and communities.

Awareness Commitment in Groups

An essential practice in all mammal groups is the sharing of awareness. Awareness Commitment is a core principle of mammal life. It's impossible for one group member to stay alert and aware all the time, so members must take turns in different states of alertness. When one member decides to rest—to lie down to sleep and deeply let go—it's serious business. Though deep rest is a concept most easily observed and learned with prey animals who live in herds, it's absolutely applicable to all mammal groups, humans included. Writer Parker Palmer says, "Self-care is never a selfish act—it is simply good stewardship of the only gift I have, the gift I was put on earth to offer others. Anytime we can listen to true self and give the care it requires, we do it not only for ourselves, but for the many others whose lives we touch."

Throughout history, a common social norm across cultures has been to share resources and roles. When we live more communally and in closer-knit families, tribes, and communities, we are more connected to how much we need each other for survival. Globally, human groups who still live or work more interdependently have shared awareness norms as part of their everyday life. You can see this in military groups, first responders, and medical teams. Sharing roles and awareness responsibility allows us to take turns keeping watch. In animal groups, awareness is a herd phenomenon. It moves through the herd as a shared resource and is the most efficient way for a group to stay safe, cohesive, and attend to energy conservation. Being "on call" for awareness is an invisible baton that is passed all day, every day. Ideally, mammals remain in a "calm alert" state and individual members take shifts in awareness leadership. A "calm alert" state is the most sustainable for the mammal nervous system. We take turns noticing things and communicating to the group if needed. Whoever is on duty in their awareness role allows the others to rest and their nervous systems to relax. Groups thrive because they share this responsibility.

Awareness Fatigue

Awareness Fatigue occurs when too many people rely on one person to stay alert and that individual vacillates between micromanaging and exhaustion, neither of which make them effective in awareness. How many among us have designed our lives so that we sign up for awareness without getting breaks for rest? It's a common human problem! When we aren't sharing awareness, we are usually swinging wildly between hypervigilance and being "checked out." The problem with this pattern is that we are sending signals to our fellow mammals that we aren't reliable herd members. We may take on these tactical roles but, as mammals, we can see through the incompetency, and we won't trust the individual with awareness fatigue. This is because they aren't trustworthy! Usually, groups put the burden of awareness on one or two people and they become symptomatic: irritable, anxious, tired, overwhelmed, and overworked. They act like martyrs, yet they are not valued in their groups. Another common problem is that the awareness leader is on duty but does not share what they notice. They don't tell the truth about what they see. Humans struggle to give timely, honest feedback to improve the health of the group. Safe groups are committed to sharing awareness and communicating about what the group needs.

The Busy Disease

Sometimes we are not so gently thrust into awareness. We might hit an internal tipping point with stress, or what I call The Busy Disease of human doing, loneliness, boredom, and emptiness. Or sometimes we get feedback from others that we aren't hitting the mark in our relationships. Someone can't connect with us as deeply as they wish. When we are living with The Busy Disease, over time our lives begin to lose vibrancy or our relationships fade. We keep ourselves moving and overwhelmed with tasks, overscheduled to the extreme, which prevents us from tuning in and around. On autopilot, we become quite numb to the harm and pain of The Busy Disease. We are suffering but we don't even know it.

Awareness Is a Choice

Waking up our Natural Leadership Awareness is a powerful choice, but the decision to engage with awareness is just the first step. Remember, like many of our mammal traits, awareness is a capacity. If we don't practice and cultivate our awareness, it lies mostly dormant. To expand this awareness capacity and integrate the Four Channels of Natural Leadership Awareness, we really have to commit to exercise this part of us as much as possible. At first, it can feel tiring and even a bit burdensome. Reflect on this choice and become more conscious and intentional about how it may serve you. These are some reflective questions that can help:

- Why is it important for you to be more aware and awake in your life?
- What are you at risk of missing if you give up your awareness?
- Is it important for the people in your life to be more awake and aware? Is that something you long for?
- How might your relationships be different if you were more aware?
- What is the hardest part of committing to more awareness?
- If you become more aware, what are you afraid you might notice?

How to Tune Your Awareness Instrument

You are the instrument of how you live, work, and relate with others. Your knowledge, wisdom, compassion, empathy, skills, tools, intuition, body, and relational capacities comprise what we can call The Instrument of You. Imagine yourself as a rare violin. When it rests in the soft velvet of its case, its strings naturally relax. When it's time to play again, it needs to be tuned. The beauty of its notes relies on attention, adjustment, and fine-tuning.

As relational beings, we must tune ourselves as an ongoing practice. Regardless of how we work with others, our emotional leadership and relational preparedness take an intentional effort in order to keep "our side of the street clear of our own debris." We all have baggage. We carry with us a kind of residue of our own making—other people's baggage that we have unconsciously agreed to carry and/or emotional and relational patterns that have affected and shaped us.

If we work and live with other humans, we have a responsibility to become aware of who we are, to know our most vulnerable areas, to have an ongoing plan for how to engage support, and to practice tuning our own instrument. As teachers, trainers, coaches, therapists, managers, parents, friends and family, and community members, we will unconsciously be impacted by all that we have experienced—good, bad, and neutral.

Thinking Patterns
- What are some of your negative thinking patterns?
- Do you have any blind spots or denial systems to watch for?
- Do you have any deep-seated beliefs that can get in the way of listening objectively to others? How can you account for those so that you can be helpful?
- What does it sound like when your ego has taken over your thinking?

Triggers
- What are your most tender emotional spots?
- What are some relational patterns that are most upsetting?
- In your history, what are your most powerful injuries?
- Are any of your triggers active, and if so, what do you need to do to reduce emotional inflammation?

Body Tension or Pain
- Where do you hold tension in your body?
- What does it tell you about what is needed or not needed?
- Have you been holding any pain that might need attention or be trying to signal to you?
- What kind of physical behaviors do you do when your body is sending you important messages about your needs or the needs of others?
- What does your body need in order to release tension and rest?

Stress or Pressure
- When you are under too much stress, what do you do?
- Are you feeling an excess of pressure, and if so, what can you do to lessen it?
- How does stress impact how you show up in your relationships?

Instincts/Primitive Drives
- When you consider your human animal instincts, which ones do you most commonly access? How do they get you into trouble?
- Are any of your primitive drives especially excitable right now? If so, what can you do to help them settle?

Natural Leadership Gifts
- In your relationships, what is your most unique leadership contribution?
- Do you overuse it and get yourself into trouble?

- How can you stay aware of this tendency so that you protect that aspect of yourself and/or you don't overstep what is needed with others?

Once you have a more general sense of how the instrument of you falls out of tune, you can become more efficient and skilled at tuning it. The goal here is to work on Awareness Channel One—yourself—so that you can interact with others and the world around you with the best parts of you leading.

The Practice: Noticing Things

Noticing Things, as a practice, allows us to hone our Natural Leadership Awareness so that we can use some of our instincts to bring more joy into our lives. This can be a way to engage with the world around us and to have a deeper connection to the world within. Noticing Things has the potential to make you a cranky perfectionist. But if you train your eye in a different way and use it to see with a softer, gentler lens, you can look for the good, look for what is interesting, and look for what lights you up inside.

Start with a daily practice of finding extraordinary beauty and slowing down enough to find meaning in the ordinary. Here's how you do it:

1. Keep it simple.
2. Create a routine, a certain time of day to practice.
3. Create some structure like an alarm so that you remember to do it.
4. Slow down and look around. Notice what you notice.
5. Let your body and your curiosity tell you what lights you up, excites you, draws you in.

6. Snap a photo.

7. Pause and ask yourself a few questions: How does this image make me feel? What does it ask me to think about? How can it guide me today?

CHAPTER THREE

Scope

How much an observant man might learn by an accurate and systematic examination of all that came his way.
SHERLOCK HOLMES

Contexts control our behavior, and our mindsets determine how we interpret each context.
ELLEN LANGER

Once internalized, an ecological perspective cannot be ignored. When one has stepped inside the ecosystemic paradigm and become aware of the systemic processes involved in all human and environmental dynamics, one cannot be made unaware.
JAMES MADDOCK AND NOEL LARSON

The Story: My Junkyard Dog

The trail is brutal. You can see it and feel it right away. It's like a steep staircase built into the side of the mountain, redwood trees hovering and crowding, their immense height almost offensive even in their dramatic beauty. You know it's a tough trail when these gorgeous giants seem like an assault to your personal space. Hardship, whether physical or emotional, can elicit this struggle in us, so consuming that only pure, unfiltered aggression can propel us forward. I squint my eyes at the trees and hate them a little. The dogs are unfazed and doubling or tripling my steps. Up and down and back again, they use my lagging pace to their advantage, bouncing around this torture trail like it's a canine trampoline.

We get to a false summit, a ridgeline where the trail opens and flattens. I'm panting and the dogs are smiling. I can feel my posture straighten out and all of the tension of the climb begins to release. I know we'll be heading up the mountain again soon, but for now, I can enjoy the openness. We're headed slightly downhill, and I see a small group of hikers approaching with two black labs bounding forward. "They're super friendly!" one woman shouts in our direction. From my somewhat elevated spot in the terrain, I get a good view of the whole scene. The trail is about to tighten into a singletrack again, and this human and canine group seems a bit unruly. The woman yells again, "Our dogs love other dogs!" I notice her volume. She's using retractable leashes and the dogs are tangled in each other's leashes and also getting caught on branches along the trail. She's fumbling around trying to get a hold of them, but these beasts are big and she seems unable to get the leash lengths to retract.

I slow down. I'm watching. I make a quiet clicking sound, which gets my dogs' attention. Just under my breath, I whisper, "Here." All three dogs circle back to my feet and we come to a stop together. I continue to observe and listen. The woman is still scrambling with dog leashes as her thundering greetings fill the forest. Her words and her face are friendly. Her labs look friendly too. But their energy is giant and feels like a runaway train headed in our direction. Georgie and Glen are paying attention but seem more curious than stressed. Tyler, on the other hand, is entirely worried. The muscles around his shoulders are tense and his hackles are up. It's like you can see his fight-or-flight system gearing up. I feel the contagion of this in my own body. I'm worrying about Tyler worrying.

I don't have enough time to leash my dogs, but they are accustomed to listening and staying with me with or without leashes. We walk off the trail and head about twenty feet into a lush mess of ferns. We keep slowly moving, making a wide arc as we move. I put myself between the dogs and the trail as the hikers and dogs pass us.

"We can let them meet and greet! Mine love playing in the forest!"

This lady is not giving up.

"Stay with me. We're okay," I whisper to my pack. "Hope you all have a great walk!" I say to the group as we complete the arc and make our way back to the trail.

Tyler stays sidled against my leg, so close I'm afraid I might step on his paws or trip over him. All of us are back on the dirt path and I release the invisible leash, our commitment to proximity unfettered with one word.

"Okay," I say.

The dogs scatter and go bounding as the trail slopes upward and we begin another climb. Tyler runs and then pauses. He shakes himself off, his whole body waving from side to side. You can almost see the tension flying from his fur. He turns around with an open mouth, relaxed, almost smiling. We look each other in the eye, and I tell him he's a good boy. This is progress—for both of us.

I met Tyler when my dear friend Nicky got him as a puppy. I spent many long afternoons with Nicky while training our dogs together. She had taken me under her wing and mentored me in sheepherding. It was great to have a friend with decades of both Border Collie and livestock experience. Nicky was a natural teacher. With friends I've made through animals, I've found a few of those relationships that run deep and go way beyond our common animal interests. Nicky was one of those people. We met through the dogs, but our time together covered big-ticket topics like marriage, parenting, and spirituality. We'd work our dogs, focus on the training with as much intensity as their piercing collie eyes, but then we would rest in the shade and consider life's many questions, share stories, and quietly but powerfully support each other.

Nicky raised Tyler, and they enjoyed a lovely partnership until Nicky's untimely death. Only two months after her husband passed away from a long cancer journey, Nicky became ill and died just weeks later. Her condition declined so rapidly that a diagnosis was never fully determined. No doubt the heartbreak of losing her lifelong love played a role. Tyler was about four years old at the time, and within weeks, he lost both of his primary people as well as his home. After a few months living with another friend, Tyler was offered to me. I was honored to take him in, with the condition that he got along with my daughter, Emma, and with our dog, Glen. It felt like a tribute to Nicky.

Tyler fit right in. His sweet nature and comical Border Collie quirks were a great addition to the ranch. As is the case with all mammals, it takes some time and experiences before you really know each other. Tyler and I worked our way through each other's layers, and it didn't take long before we fell in love. Nicky's husband had been ill for years, and her hands were full taking care of him, their ranch, and their many animals. Tyler was beautifully trained for working sheep, but I got the sense he hadn't done much off the ranch. He loved meeting people, but he was awkward and quite insecure in new places and downright troubled with dogs he didn't know. He even had a disastrous vet visit, which resulted in him being double muzzled and getting a "dangerous dog" label on his medical record.

I've always prided myself in raising dogs who are good citizens, so I have to admit that my experience with Tyler was perplexing and humbling. I was out of my comfort zone entirely. We would do our daily walks in the hills surrounding the ranch, and Tyler would snarl at the end of the leash when we passed others. When we walked by a fence with another dog, Tyler was like a halibut thrashing to get free from a fishing line. This sweet-faced and smiling dog would go from mild to wild in what seemed to be a heartbeat. I got sucked into Tyler's drama very quickly, and what was his became ours. It started with confusion, not understanding what was causing his upset and not knowing what to do to fix it. But once my ego got involved, we were off to the races. Emotional contagion is a thing for mammals. It doesn't matter if we are different species, emotions carry from one limbic system to another in seconds. We are symbiotic by nature, and we mirror each other's experiences for the purposes of empathy, attuning to our inner worlds so we know how to care for one another and to sense danger when it exists.

I don't know if I was feeling protective of Tyler, myself, the other dogs we encountered, or the situation as a whole, but Tyler's snarls, growls, and lunges brought out heated emotions in me. I vacillated between fury toward the jerk dogs who I believed were provoking my loving and kind dog and indignation directed at Tyler for being naughty and rude. I was in a blame trap, looking to nail whoever was at fault for all of the disturbance. We couldn't take a peaceful walk without hitting at least one emotional pothole. I was at one end of the leash and Tyler was at the other, and we were like two junkyard dogs charging at the world. It seemed to come from nowhere, these explosions of his. My conclusion: Tyler was dog-aggressive, and most other dogs were bullies and just making things worse. Even though I kept coming back to this narrative, something about it felt off. I knew, in what I like to call my "knower," that there was more to the story. I was too close to the problem because I had gotten pulled deep into the emotional undertow.

When I first started working dogs on vast and open hills, a powerful and life-changing awareness began to emerge. It was on top of one of those hills that I got to see a dog experience the power of perspective. I had been training a young dog named Cash, trying for months to get him to stay balanced on the whole flock of sheep, but he would pick out one surly ewe and obsess about her. Meanwhile, the rest of the flock was unattended, and they would begin to scatter. He would quickly get frustrated, and nearly every time, it would end with him dive-bombing the sheep, everyone going in different directions in complete chaos. We hit a wall in the training, and the scenario was becoming more routine, which meant it was in danger of becoming a habit. Once we had the hills to help, my dog had a different vantage point. He was able to see and experience "the big picture." The hill taught him that staying back gave him a superpower. If he kept a distance, space became a resource. He could see more. He had scope.

It's hard to convince a dog, or any mammal for that matter, to let go of control. A Border Collie wants to manage a flock of sheep the same way a parent wants to manage children, a teacher their students, or a corporate executive their team. We feel the pressure, and we react. We jump in, often with our egos and stories triggered and smoldering. Rather than assessing, choosing, and calmly influencing, we see a problem and we are pulled into it. But when we can learn to wait, to pause, and to let things unfold, we can actually see more clearly. We gain a full view of the situation and can then choose how we want to step in. We can strategize and effect change with more stability. Just a little space and time—a pause—can make all the difference.

With Tyler, scope came to me in a flash. I was walking the dogs by one of our problem fences. Thinking of the last time we had a fence scuffle, I had a feeling of dread. I noticed my hands tense as I clenched Tyler's leather leash. It's me. I'm starting it. I was anticipating the problem, my mind and body were mobilizing, and I was clearly sending alarm signals to my dog. I was creating, or at least co-creating the overreaction to stress. I thought of the magic question that my mentor, Jim, taught me when I was becoming a therapist: What's happening right now? What was I doing with my body, my mind? What was the story I was carrying about Tyler? The question allowed me to zoom out, to study all of the parts at play. Where were my dogs in relation to me? What was happening for Tyler? For Glen? What was the traffic like on the street? What were the other dogs doing in their yard? What time of day was it? What season? Suddenly, my vantage point has shifted. I had scope, and with it, I could observe the environment and all of us in it. These questions allowed me to see the whole. I could see my part and my role.

I didn't create the problem per se; however, by naming it as a problem and blaming it on Tyler, I was not able to see what was out of balance in our interspecies pack. Each time we walked, I focused on the problem, became tense, and added this powerful storyline: Tyler is dog-aggressive. Tyler is bad on the leash. Tyler is .

.. Tyler is . . . Tyler is . . . This story put all of the pressure on Tyler, which was the last thing he needed when he was already feeling so much stress and fear. The dogs were needing something different from me, but I would never be able to see what was needed if I was directly on top of the problem and emotionally dysregulated. Glen, because of his temperament and life experiences, was able to tolerate me being a more distracted (and perhaps lazy) pack member. But Tyler needed more from me. It was time for me to grow. It was not about training Tyler to be better on the leash or improve his behavior with other dogs. Tyler didn't need to be "fixed." He needed me to show up. He needed a more mature and stable leader.

I stayed in my position with scope and could see our relationship in a new light. Tyler was still new to me. We didn't have a solid foundation of trust yet. He turned to me for support, but I wasn't showing up for him. I was walking him and talking on the phone or lost in thought, daydreaming or admiring birds, flowers, or gazing at clouds. I wasn't holding my Awareness Commitment, and for an insecure mammal, I was failing in my leadership role. There is an implicit agreement between mammals about who is going to lead or hold awareness. Tyler didn't feel prepared for this. He barely knew the world outside the ranch where he had grown up. He was looking to me for support, and I wasn't there. When things became stressful, I would join his emotional upset, jumping into the mess, hollering, hurrying off, and sending him a message that the dog encounters were unsafe. Really, I was showing him that the whole world was unsafe.

It took a leap of faith and a decision to do the complete opposite of what I had been doing with Tyler. Instead of gripping the leather, rushing past stressful situations, and shouting at Tyler or the other dogs, I committed to slow down and to let go. I had to learn to stay. And that would help Tyler learn to stay. The practice of staying is at the heart of learning scope. The energy of the moment has tremendous power. It's all too easy to get pulled into it without our doing. Learning to stay is about holding the tension so I can remain in my own stability and to observe, a bit like withstanding a strong wind and not getting blown over.

I did something symbolic and terrifying. I started holding Tyler's leash between my index finger and my thumb. Instead of a closed and white-knuckled fist, I just let the leash rest gently as if I was carrying the wing of a butterfly and trying not to damage its delicate membrane. I planned ahead and put myself between Tyler and any stressors in the world. The message to him was: I've got your back. I moved slowly and calmly. I breathed. I said out loud, "We're good. I've got this, my friend." The junkyard dog in me didn't need to bark and threaten to bite. In fact, instead of viciousness, I felt a protective love that was much more peaceful and sustainable. It soothed me. And I could feel that it settled my dogs. It was a complete and immediate turnaround for Tyler. He looked to me, and I was there. I was staying. My stride was calm and steady. My body was soft and strong at the same time. I was holding my scope, holding my commitment to my pack, and holding my own leadership in a way that would change my dog walks forever.

The Concept: Scope and the Big Picture

All living things are part of larger systems. Scope is an essential and primitive part of our survival instincts and is a central concept and tool in the Natural Leadership model, allowing us to see "the big picture" of a system at any given moment. A broader perspective allows us to observe and understand the world around us and to assess what might be out of balance or what is needed. While humans are particularly well-built for scope because of our brain's capacity for executive functioning, all mammals use scope to some degree in order to assess their environments for safety or for activities like hunting. Birds of prey use treetops and flight to maintain scope for hunting. In the wolf pack, the leader of the pack stays far behind the rest of the wolves to observe the group, protect, and oversee needs. The human herd uses scope for our basic survival needs; however, scope also allows us to think critically, problem-solve, establish context, create strategy, and make meaning. We access scope so that we can evaluate what is happening, attend to change or pressure, and make choices about how to care for ourselves and others. Imagine trying to steer a ship around icebergs without the knowledge of what is below the surface of the water. We use scope to see the whole view.

What Is a System?

A system is a group of interrelated parts in process that form an interdependent whole. Some basic examples of systems include: an automobile, a forest, a human body, a nuclear family, a team, or a herd of horses. Each system has a process, pattern, and/or theme that describes how it works. A system is surrounded and influenced by its internal parts and by its environment. If one part of a system is not functioning well or not working at all, it affects the whole system. Consider the human body and the cascade effect if something like a nasal passage has a significant block. The lack of airflow can lead to trouble breathing while exercising or snoring while sleeping. Snoring can lead to sleep apnea, which can affect blood flow in the brain. This can lead to a neurological event like a stroke. When one part of a system changes, it predictably affects the system as a whole.

For our purposes, we are interested in relational systems and the way that individuals and groups are interconnected and affect one another. Using scope in our human relationships allows us to be more strategic and solution-oriented. Without scope, we chase problems and end up masking symptoms rather than influencing a relationship to grow and develop. Author and systems theorist William Tate writes about this, "The component parts of a system, especially including leadership, can be best understood in the context of relationships with other parts of the system and other systems, rather than in isolation." When we can maintain scope, especially as a leader of any kind of group, we can see themes emerge and can make intentional choices about how and where to step in.

How Scope Helps Us

Maintaining the "big picture" perspective gives us the space and time we need to assess our surroundings. Whether it's needed or not, our animal body awareness utilizes brain functioning to collect data about our safety. When we use scope as a practice, we dedicate focus to an instinct function so that we can do it more efficiently and use information from our evaluation to determine our next moves. Scope gives us a new way of looking at the world.

About this, my mentor, Jim Maddock, and his wife, psychologist, Noel Larson write, "Like putting on a pair of glasses and seeing the world more clearly, one comes to depend upon the view that is built into the lenses. The mind now 'knows' how the world can be perceived, and things viewed through the glasses become very difficult to disregard. Thus, taking an ecological approach is largely a matter of adding layers of recognition and making use of these in particular ways."

Looking at ourselves within a system and thinking critically about systems also helps us to see beyond symptoms. Imagine if you went to the doctor and said you had a sore throat, and your doctor diagnosed your sore throat and treated it before asking any other questions or examining your ears or your lungs. The sore throat exists, but it's just a sign that your body's system is out of balance. Whether it's a physical system like a body, machine, or factory, or a relational system like a family, team, or classroom, it's easy and typical to see a symptom and focus on only that. But we can train ourselves to think beyond a more pathological, symptom-focused worldview and pivot to a paradigm more aligned with the laws of nature. All living systems are attempting to find and maintain homeostasis or balance. What this means is that signs and symptoms of trouble are often movements and efforts toward solution. So, if we can slow down and investigate what we see as "wrong," it will point us to what wants to come into equilibrium. When we can name themes in a system, we can form a hypothesis about what is happening. Then we can experiment with effecting change.

Our inner mammal loves when we have the opportunity to see and feel scope because:

- We are able to discover a system's dynamics, conditions, and limitations.
- We can make choices about what we want to do or what is needed.
- The position allows us to make choices rather than react.
- The perspective and vantage point allows us to notice patterns and themes.
- We are better able to cope with stressors.

When We Lose Scope

When we lose our scope, we dive into high-pressure situations, also known as problems, and we become part of them. With emotional reactivity and our survival instincts at play, we are no longer able to make choices about how we want to influence or what role we want to play. In fact, when we are relationally upset, we lose our space for influence. A very common example of this occurs when children tantrum. Because our empathy system is so powerful, parents are vulnerable to joining the tantrum. It happens all the time. We get right on top of the dysregulation, and in just seconds, we have the experience of being trapped. It's like we have nowhere to move so we get rigid and reactive. We've become part of the system, and we can't see clearly. When we become frustrated, angry, or fearful, we lose our emotional leadership and can no longer be a force of stability. Instincts and natural capacities like empathy are a huge asset to the human herd but are most powerfully used when we have more consciousness about them. We don't want our instincts to be fully in charge. Rather, it's much more helpful if the instincts inform and we use scope to discern and respond with more balance. Scope allows us the time and space to take the information from our primitive signal system and use it with conscious choice.

Why We Give Up Scope

Predatory mammals who are built for activities like hunting need to be able to hyper-focus in order to survive. We all know what it's like to get pulled into a certain task or activity and to miss all other details happening around us. When this happens, we temporarily lose our scope and are operating with all kinds of blind spots. We succumb to stress or tension, pressure or anxiety in the moment because we want to change it. Even if we haven't figured out what it is, our brain says: *Make it stop!*

As leaders, parents, teachers, therapists, and coaches, we are also propelled into a helper role, and this tendency toward rescue will cause us to lose our scope. We jump in because we want to relieve others from their suffering as soon as possible. Our empathy is on high volume, and we don't like how *we* feel as we feel the pain of others. So, we want to make it go away before learning what it is. Other times, we jump in because we feel pressure to perform. Others come to us and want us to fix things for them, and we take on that task, thinking we are supposed to be miracle workers and that we had better fix things before they give up on us and think we're incompetent. As parents, we might jump in when we're in public because our children are being atrocious and it's a huge embarrassment to us. We don't want to be judged by others, so we dive into fix-it mode.

Using Scope to Cope

As we practice using scope, its benefits as an emotional regulator begin to be felt and known. Not at first though! In fact, pausing and staying can be excruciating. We're working against a tidal wave of emotion and instinct. Waiting is a skill. On my daughter's first day of preschool, she came home and reported, "Mommy! I learned how to stand in line and wait." As we tolerate the discomfort of holding scope, we gain more confidence in our own self-leadership. We can manage ourselves and our anxiety, and this makes us much more effective in our leadership roles. Rather than throwing our dysregulated selves into the middle of a conflict, we can be a force of calm and approach situations with the notion that those involved have within them the ability to find balance.

Managing Inherent Anxiety and Pressure with Scope

Change, in any part of a system, negative or positive, affects other parts of the system, and the system as a whole. Change creates pressure, and pressure creates change. The mammal nervous system experiences pressure from its internal and external environments. Pressure and anxiety exist on a continuum and range from barely noticed to completely flooded and overwhelmed.

Pressure is inherent in all systems and is a part of life and relationships. In fact, pressure is the necessary ingredient for change. Our physical and relational systems need to heat up and/or have enough pressure for change to occur. It's like a chemistry crucible, made of strong enough metal or clay to hold the heat of a chemical reaction so that the elements can transform. Humans, as individual systems or in interpersonal systems, experience high-pressure situations and symptoms that precipitate change. Scope allows us to work with anxiety and pressure instead of trying to stop the inevitable. It is a soothing space that allows us to tolerate change by examining it and using our higher brain functioning to make meaning out of it.

How to See the Big Picture

Think of a challenge or issue you are facing at home or with your work. Pick something juicy that really has you feeling stuck.

I bet you can start to feel that obsessive pull toward it. Imagine rolling hills covered in sheep. You know that you have a bit of that Border Collie desire for control in you! We all do. Go to the top of the hill and give yourself the gift of scope. Ask yourself these questions:

- Am I too close to the problem?
- If I change my vantage point, what information do I begin to see?
- Am I about to blow things up by putting too much pressure on others?
- Where is the pressure coming from?

The Practice: Take the Roof Off

For this exercise, you will need to identify a laboratory of sorts. You need a group to observe. This could be a group of coworkers or colleagues, a bunch of children playing in a park or learning in a classroom, a family at a restaurant, a team in a meeting, or even a group of dogs at the dog park or a herd of horses.

You are going to put on your anthropologist hat, sit back, and watch. Remember to maintain your scope. You can't get involved or you will lose your ability to study the system. One of the best ways to keep your scope is to imagine that you are taking the roof off a building and peering inside and from above. Vantage point is key here.

Take some field notes. Use the "big picture" perspective to see what you see. Use the information you gather to identify themes and begin to define what this system is all about.

- What are the people/animals doing? How are they inter-acting with each other?
- What is the tone/texture/feel of the interactions?
- If you tune in to your human animal instrument, what do you feel in your body as you observe?
- In one to two sentences, try to describe the culture of the group. What is the main theme of the group?
- What, if anything, seems out of balance? Describe what it is.
- Remember that systems are always trying to find balance. What behaviors do you notice that may be attempts to rebalance the whole system?
- You aren't going to intervene or influence. But if you were going to enter this system, what kind of support does it most need? What kind of support does it least need?

CHAPTER FOUR

Pressure

The soul is like a wild animal—tough, resilient, savvy, self-sufficient and yet exceedingly shy. If we want to see a wild animal, the last thing we should do is to go crashing through the woods, shouting for the creature to come out. But if we are willing to walk quietly into the woods and sit silently for an hour or two at the base of a tree, the creature we are waiting for may well emerge, and out of the corner of an eye we will catch a glimpse of the precious wildness we seek.

PARKER PALMER

The Story: My Guru Is a Bay Mare

He hopped off the bay mare, the smooth leather of his saddle seat shining, empty, and almost calling to me. He knelt down to tinker with a broken sprinkler in the sandy arena. The moment hit me between the eyes. The words were out of my mouth before I even knew what I was saying, "Can I ride her?" He stood up and looked at me with raised eyebrows. "Get off your horse," he said, and I swung my leg over Rosie's back. I couldn't get to his mare fast enough. Maybe I was afraid he'd change his mind. Maybe I was afraid I'd change mine. I put my foot in the stirrup, grabbed a handful of her black mane, and thrust myself above her. The sprinkler started again, the rush of water like a snare drum. I felt a couple of drops hit my face. *I'm very awake. I'm very awake right now.*

I met Sally when she was a youngster, just a slight filly fresh off the trailer. Not long before, I had purchased my lovely horse, Rosie, and was knee-deep in our love affair when Sally arrived at the barn where I rode at that time. Just your average bay mare, brown coat with a thick, black mane and tail. But there was something special in her eye and how she looked at you and through you. Her eye called for attention and asked you to listen and also open yourself completely. After some time in my relationship with Rosie, I had come to trust my instincts in noticing a certain spark in horses. I sought it in all of my animals, this verve and aliveness that makes individuals more committed to connection. A vivacious eye sees all there is to see. Mammals with this quality have a presence that captures the attention of others, a self-leadership that makes you want to be near them just to be near them. I noticed it right away when I first saw Sally—and it shot straight to my heart.

I admired her from afar, kind of like a childhood crush. I would periodically stop to say hello and to give her a friendly rub. Sally was owned by Billy, who was my horse trainer at the time. He had many horses of his own, and he rode her periodically, but she mostly rotated through droves of riders and other students. For years, I watched her, rode next to her, passed her stall, and my interest in her lingered each time I encountered her. I continued my deep soul connection with my Rosie. Yet I couldn't help but feel a pull toward Sally. That pull lasted for years, and it landed in me in the saddle riding her for the first time. The rest was just a series of open doors, those decisions you come to and it's clear there's really no decision at all. It's just a matter of putting one foot in front of the other. I'm on the fence about the concept of fate. I'm a realist with a strong connection to a higher power. But I am awestruck by what presents itself. Sally presented herself. That empty saddle presented itself. The opportunity for our partnership had arrived.

When I took Sally home to my ranch, something shifted. A story was born as is often the case with humans. That busy meaning maker will spin a tale no matter what. I had years of data about Sally swirling about in my mind. She lived in a box stall, and I was saddened because she seemed lonely and bored. She had cycled through dozens of riders. I had seen her trained hard and had even ridden in the same show ring. The story I told myself grew, and it quickly became a web I found myself tangled in. The story took on a life of its own, and it carried a huge weight in my heart. It also occupied a huge amount of mental energy. I needed to help Sally, to relieve her stress and pressure from her life as a performance horse. I would restore her natural balance so she could be herself. I would set her spirit free.

Sally kept a distance from me. It was subtle but always there. I would pick up the lead rope and she'd hesitate before walking behind me. I'd gather the reins and she would brace, holding her neck stiff, and it felt like her mouth would freeze with my contact. I took it personally sometimes. I thought I was doing the relationship wrong. Other times, I just worked harder to win her over, to heal her, to soothe her, to convince her that she was going to be okay. This was a good life we would share. She just needed to open up. That story kept a confusing wall of pressure between me and my new horse for nearly three months.

One day, we were in the round pen together. It had been a good twenty minutes of interacting, and she was doing her usual all-business routine, moving about and listening to me but with her head turned away from me ever so slightly. A clear message:

No. Too much. Too much pressure. I walked alongside her maybe three times around the pen, the late afternoon sunlight glowing and sending these powerful beams through her mane. Then, something very unexpected happened. I saw my own hair glowing in the light. What occurred was one of the truest moments of my life. We walked side by side as if we were in separate but parallel channels or tracks. I had a profound sensation that we were completely connected, but I had my path and she had hers. Something unnamable opened inside of me. I could call it freedom or peace or letting go but those words diminish the experience. It was like the tectonic plates of my own personal earth shifted. I felt a smile come and some tears. We kept walking, and I could finally look straight ahead and focus on where I was headed. I knew Sally was there, so very present, but my own path finally mattered. I no longer felt compelled to focus on hers. We slowed down and walked toward each other. As equals. When we touched in that instant, our partnership was born.

That day, I broke through the story I had been carrying, and I realized it was *my* story, not Sally's. In fact, it had been a lifelong story between me and people close to me for much of my life. This horse was completely fine. More than fine, she was peaceful in the moment. But I was feeling and projecting so much pressure and worry, and Sally could feel it. The more I pressured her to be okay, the more she kept me at bay. When I let go, we could accurately see and feel each other. We could finally have an equal relationship. The pressure I was putting on her kept her away, and it kept me from experiencing myself. Sally didn't need me to fix her. She wasn't broken. And neither was I. But I finally realized how much pressure I had been living with. It wasn't just about Sally. *How long had I been carrying the narrative and all of its emotional material?*

How many relationships had it impacted? How many others did it push away? And what was the cost of me carrying it?

Glowing in the sunlight, we were witnesses to each other's wholeness. Sally's attentive eye caught mine. She could see me, and I could feel myself letting go. With each footstep in the sandy round pen, I felt lighter and more connected to myself, to a pure and free version of me. Sally held me to it, the gentlest teacher. But she insisted with a fierce love I'd never known. Her message was clear. It was time for me to take care of myself in an entirely new way, to make more space to just be.

The Concept: The Phenomenon of Pressure

The phenomenon of pressure is one that's often misunderstood. By the time humans are talking about the sensation of pressure, we are often already flooded. So, when we use the word *pressure*, we are actually talking about overwhelm, the point when our mammal organism, the human body, is already overheating. Pressure exists on a continuum and is an internal and environmental phenomenon of energy in which humans lack fluency. Our world of thought and language gets in the way of us consistently tuning in to our senses and becoming experts at how to work with things like pressure so that we can better lead our lives, moment to moment, day to day, and relationship to relationship.

The topic at hand is not about how to manage "too much pressure" but is instead about beginning to understand pressure as a primary source of information and adopting practices, behaviors, and ways of living a more aware and present life. When we work and live with others (humans or other animals), fine-tuning our awareness to pressure allows us to adjust and adapt as needed, which reduces stress and conflict and builds trust.

What Overwhelm Looks Like: A Real-Life Example

By the time you snap at a person, raise your voice, or use a harsh tone or harsh words, your pressure system has already been flooded. Your nervous system has had too many stimuli. We all know this feeling in the body. It's as if our wires fray and sparks fly. Too often, our pressure is out of balance as soon as our eyeballs see the light of day.

It might look a bit like this:

- Your day starts with a loud alarm clock.
- You put your smartphone in front of your face and start looking, reading, clicking, and scrolling.
- The news is stressful, frightening, and angering.
- You hear garbage trucks beeping and garbage cans hitting the street.
- Your dog barks.
- The neighbor's dog barks.
- Your kids won't get out of bed, and everyone is already running late.
- Your kids run in and out of your room and talk *at* you while you're trying to get dressed.
- The emails and texts start and your phone chimes every minute or two.
- The toaster bell rings, the coffee maker beeps, kid voices get louder.
- Time is passing and you are getting later and more rushed.
- You think about the fight you and your partner had yesterday.
- You feel hurt.
- You think about summer plans and financial strain.
- You think about finding a new job.

- You question your career choices and whether you've taken a wrong turn with this job.
- The car horns honk outside while you try to load the kids in the car. Your coffee spills.
- The seat belt gets stuck while the car radio blasts, and the kids argue.
- There's a traffic jam, and the clock is ticking. The kids are going to be late. So are you.
- Your phone is still chiming, and your morning workload is piling up.
- Your mother-in-law just sent a nasty text.
- Your stomach grumbles and you realize you forgot to eat.
- You take a sip of coffee and burn your tongue.

It's stressful even to read this! It's a hypothetical scenario, but humans in industrialized countries know the symptoms of this lifestyle all too well. We allow things to move too quickly, and we don't have enough space and time, a pause so our body and nervous system can catch up with what's happening around us. By the time we snap at our kids or our coworker or our negative thoughts begin to attack us, there are probably fifty or more cues that you are flooded. The body tries to tell us to adjust, to modulate before overwhelm sets in. But we don't know how to listen to pressure cues. Attuning and attending to pressure is a basic element of self-care. One of the casualties of a busy and technological modern life is that we have lost our sensitivity to pressure as a central signal system for taking care of our needs.

The Experience of Pressure as an Animal

Pressure allows mammals to feel their way through life and to adjust proximity, to negotiate sharing space, resources, and roles.

Pressure is not a good or bad phenomenon. This process of feeling the environment is not about judgment. It's just an assessment of what is happening around us and what we need to do or not do to take care of ourselves.

Interpersonally, pressure is a phenomenon of influence, the feel or a sense of persuasion that can be subtle and barely detectable—like noticing someone's mood change—or can be as severe as brute force.

Animals have maintained their sensitivity to the phenomenon of pressure in their environments, providing us a great example to learn from. This is especially true about prey animals who have to detect a whole range of pressures, including life-threatening danger, in order to stay safe. Predators enter a "zone of influence" as they begin the hunt, and the prey animal can feel or sense a shift in energy even before they can physically see it. Their survival depends on picking up invisible shifts and responding to them immediately.

Prey animals attack as a last resort. Their best defense is to sense pressure shifts or tension and flee to get out of harm's way as quickly as possible. They simply but expediently move away. When things feel "off" or suspicious, they respond by creating space from the pressure. When things feel good and safe, peaceful and settled, they rest together. Regardless of status on the food chain, together is better for all mammals. The center of the herd, or pack, is the safest and most secure place to be.

Pressure for the Human Animal

Humans have the innate capacity to feel pressure. But here is where it gets sticky. Humans insert a layer of thought and judgment on top of the pressure. The judgment gets in the way of our instincts and signals. It creates static and noise, a story that distracts us so that we can't *feel* as clearly. Sometimes we cannot get a feel for things at all. The meaning-making machine that is the human mind creates thoughts that dull and numb our sensing system, interfering with our ability to feel, assess, and attend to pressure. Our prolific thinking clouds our natural *feel* so that we don't notice pressures, and therefore we can't take care of them. Simply put, we are slow to respond to changes in our environment, and many times we don't attend to our needs at all. This is not to say that our miraculous world of thought is to be relegated. Rather, when we bring our body's natural sensory system into the equation, we can integrate pressure sensitivity into our awareness and use it with more intention. It's a basic ingredient of self-care and relational responsibility.

We live with all of these pressures we don't even know exist. Pressure is a tricky concept. It's an ever-present flow of energy in our environment, and we lean into our experiences or shut down from them depending on how much pressure we sense and how much we can tolerate. Animals and children are perfect teachers of this because their receptors to pressure are exquisitely alive and they aren't faking it through life. They feel pressure and they respond. They will immediately and unabashedly give feedback about the pressure they feel and request that others listen to their needs. Our pressure-sensing instrument is our human animal body, and we have to strip some layers of conditioning, numbing, and thinking to get better acquainted with it.

From Pressure to Numbness

Pressure without release moves through the mammal nervous system in a very specific way. Though we have varying degrees of pressure sensitivity, we share a common response to pressure.

THE PRESSURE SEQUENCE

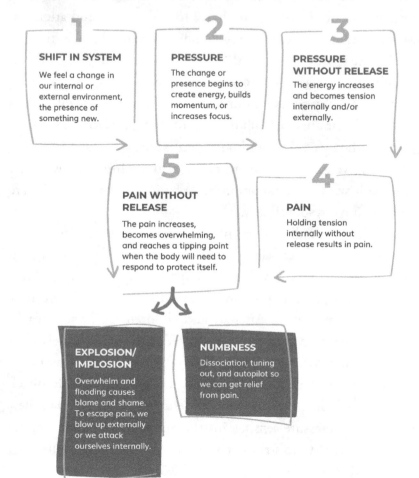

1 SHIFT IN SYSTEM

We feel a change in our internal or external environment, the presence of something new.

2 PRESSURE

The change or presence begins to create energy, builds momentum, or increases focus.

3 PRESSURE WITHOUT RELEASE

The energy increases and becomes tension internally and/or externally.

5 PAIN WITHOUT RELEASE

The pain increases, becomes overwhelming, and reaches a tipping point when the body will need to respond to protect itself.

4 PAIN

Holding tension internally without release results in pain.

EXPLOSION/ IMPLOSION

Overwhelm and flooding causes blame and shame. To escape pain, we blow up externally or we attack ourselves internally.

NUMBNESS

Dissociation, tuning out, and autopilot so we can get relief from pain.

The Consequences of Numbness

- We have less access to our mammalian signal system about safety and well-being.
- We function on autopilot and miss cues from within, from others, and from our environment.

- We experience less joy and miss cues for resources that can help us or enrich our lives.

Other Factors that Cause Insensitivity to Pressure
- Taking on too many tasks and flooding our nervous system
- Self-involvement or self-centeredness
- Emotional overwhelm
- Preoccupation with what others are doing or saying
- Justification or analysis of situations
- Using substances or behaviors to dull senses
- Pattern of ignoring signs of pressure until exploding resulting in "emotional hangover" (shame, exhaustion, numbness)

Pressure in a System
As much as we humans would like to think that change can occur with low to no conflict, stress, or effort as we skip through utopian fields of wildflowers, pressure is a natural and necessary phenomenon, and it allows us to adapt, adjust, develop, evolve, move forward, and stay healthy. Pressure is inherent in all systems and is fundamental as a life force.

Some examples of effective pressure:

- You might need to raise your voice so someone can hear you. Without enough sound waves, the vibrations won't make it to the eardrum, or the vibrations won't be strong enough.
- You need to physically press your car's accelerator to increase your speed. When the throttle is opened, air is free to fill the intake manifold, increasing the pressure. A fuel injection system adds fuel to the airflow, providing energy to the engine.

- When it's time for a child to learn a new life skill, a parent will introduce it to the child and will need to pressure them to try something unfamiliar.

Pressure also exists in order to create balance. Homeostasis refers to the state of steady conditions maintained in living systems, or a state of equilibrium for optimal functioning. In order to maintain homeostasis, systems have to adapt and adjust to pressures. Not enough pressure will result in no change. Without enough heat, the water won't boil. Too much pressure results in collapse or destruction. Think about a flooded engine, a fever that is too high and results in brain damage, or an overinflated balloon popping.

In a system, one element will experience pressure to shift in order to keep the rest of the system in balance. During infection, the immune system will cause the body to develop a fever and an increase in blood flow to bring oxygen and other immune cells to where the infection is.

In relational systems, we exert pressure on each other to move our relationships forward. We ask each other to grow. A teacher gives inspiring lectures, assigns homework, and schedules tests, all of which create pressure for students to study and learn. As a couple moves through the life cycle, one person may be inspired to seek something novel and ask their partner to join. This puts pressure on them to expand a capacity, overcome a fear, or confront an inhibition. In work settings, creativity inspires us to build and innovate, managers pressure us to work harder, and the open market pressures companies to produce and improve.

How to Study Your Pressure System

Because pressure is such a misunderstood phenomenon for human animals, it's important that we study it closely and become more aware of how it affects us. Doing a pressure audit can help us to better understand our own unique pressure system. The process helps us to look at internal sources of pressure like our emotions, beliefs, thoughts, and physical habits, as well as our external sources such as daily schedules, work expectations, or parenting responsibilities. These are the things in our environment that come in contact with our inner mammal experience and impact how much we can sustain and maintain. By doing the pressure audit for multiple days at a time, we're able to see our patterns.

This is not an exact science. Rather, it is a subjective understanding of our personal experience, offering us broad brushstrokes that can inform how we might make changes to have more ease in our lives. It can help to do this work with a coach, a group, or an accountability partner, a friend who can offer some objective input. Also, another person can ask questions that might help us become more aware of our pressure system and how it impacts our lives.

We are looking for the blatant imbalance. Too much pressure and we really squeeze and corner the human animal. It's as if the body, mind, and spirit are in a vice grip. This is the precursor to stress or pain, which ultimately result in numbness. When we consistently load up our pressure system, we live with tension and stress, which have profound consequences on our physical, mental, and relational health. Conversely, if we don't have enough pressure, we simply can't move forward, develop, and progress in our lives. Pressure can influence us in a positive way.

Pressure is what drives us, internally and externally. It's how we create, how we innovate, evolve, and grow. Pressure, when it's in balance, is a beautiful thing. Every human animal is different in terms of our sensitivities. We come into the world with a temperament, and that temperament is affected by the environment we grow up in. Each of us is born with a unique innate nature. Our relationships and environmental circumstances affect our nature. Once we're adults, those two factors are fairly well-baked into who we are. When we do a pressure audit, we discover that there isn't a one-size-fits-all approach to finding pressure balance. We're trying to find the right amount of pressure for each of us.

Where there is pressure, there are often blockages. We can think of the times when we hold a lot of tension in one area of our body. When we do so, it affects the muscles, circulation, joints, nerves, and movement. We each have certain areas of our body where we hold pressure. When it's inside the body, we usually call it tension. When we repeat the holding of tension over time, it often becomes a physical habit and may start to create a blockage in the muscles, like a knot, affecting our circulation and movement and inhibiting us from being able to walk or conduct basic activities without pain or inhibition.

Too much pressure in our thinking can also create a blockage in the mind. Let's say we are doing a lot of negative thinking about the future, i.e., worrying. Those cognitive patterns create pressure and tension, and our thinking becomes rigid. Any time we think about doing something new or consider a future event, we'll have a whole series of blockages or thought patterns that get in the way of moving forward. We won't take certain risks or actions based on that negative thinking pattern because the worry blockage is in the way.

We might have a blockage in our emotional space if we have some hurt feelings. Let's say a relationship we cared about ended and we are feeling grief. We hold pressure in our emotional system. This can prevent us from connecting with others, opening our hearts, or taking relational risks. Until we heal, clear that blockage, and release that emotional pressure, we aren't open for business, and our relationships suffer as a result.

When we work with others, relating or leading in any capacity, we can fine-tune our sensitivity to pressure and use it to notice where people have too little or too much pressure. If you study other animals in their groups, they use pressure all day long in order to create movement, get out of stuck spots, avoid danger, signal times of rest, protect, to pursue basic needs, and to navigate and share space.

The Practice: Your Pressure Audit

The purpose of a pressure audit is to gain clarity about pressures in our daily lives. The more aware we are about pressure, the better we can adjust and shape our routines and relationships. Adjusting to pressure is one of the fundamentals of self-care. A pressure audit is best done during a concentrated period so that we can track patterns. Try using it for five to seven days, preferably at the middle or end of the day. Keep track of your daily pressure results in order to study the data. Any pressure point that has a six or higher rating is an indicator of an area for which you need more self-care.

RATE YOUR PRESSURE ACCORDING TO THIS SCALE

0	1	2	3	4	5
NO PRESSURE	A LOW HUM	CREATES ENERGY	MOTIVATES MOVEMENT	SUSTAINS ACTION	A BIT OF URGENCY

6	7	8	9	10	
HOLDING TENSION	FEELINGS OF OVERWHELM	FEELING FLOODED	PAIN AND STRESS	NUMB	

HUMAN ANIMAL PRESSURE POINTS	PRESSURE QUESTION	PRESSURE RATING
THE BODY	Tension in your muscles?	
	Aches and pains?	
	Low energy with high activity demand?	
	Amount of rest?	
	Amount of movement or body exertion?	
	Amount of physical contact and/or affection?	
THE MIND	Worried thoughts about the future?	
	Questions about your efficiency or worthiness?	
	Thoughts are negative and/or critical?	
	Dwelling on past events and regrets?	
THE HEART	Carrying around hurt, emotional pain, or grief?	
	Feeling afraid, nervous, or panicked?	
	Quick to anger, irritation, or rage?	
THE SPIRIT	Enough meaning and purpose in your days?	
	Time/space for quiet reflection?	
	Connected to a greater force outside of yourself?	
BASIC NEEDS	Preoccupied with worry about food or shelter?	
	Physical or mental health?	
	Struggling to make financial ends meet or insecurity or instability at work?	
YOUR RELATIONAL NEEDS	Focused on caring for others?	
	Others are supporting you and you accept support?	
	Feelings of loneliness or isolation?	
	Enough time alone and without interruption?	
	Felt genuinely seen and/or heard?	

CHAPTER FIVE

Pace

Between stimulus and response, there is a space. In that space
lies our freedom and power to choose our response. In our
response lies our growth and freedom.

VIKTOR FRANKL

Adopt the pace of nature: her secret is patience.

RALPH WALDO EMERSON

The Story: The Busy Disease

You can hear the wind move through their tails, thick horsehair
playing a few simple notes, the faintest melody as the air moves
through each strand. I've stood next to horses my whole life, quietly, paying attention. But I've never noticed the song in their
tails. This is a first. We're under the big pine. Its needles make
music too, a metallic hush like a snare drum. I close my eyes and
the sounds move from ear to ear. I hear the long breath of my
equine friend nearest to me. It's always a reminder. I breathe too.

It's been pouring for weeks, it seems. But we've had a few days
of sun, and the mud has dried enough to walk over without sink-

ing into it and sloshing about. These are my favorite days. The grass and soil drink up the rainwater. At times, I can hear that too. The herd has taught me to be quiet enough and slow enough to notice these things. Noticing things. This is my original gift. It's always been there but I didn't have full access to it with so much static in my mind. I have it back now. I see and feel so much more.

We've been meandering together for a while now, the horses and me. I follow their rhythms. I stay with them, in proximity. Each animal exists on their own. There are six of them. Yet the herd itself, the group, is its own animal, a system of parts that operates as one. The herd is like a body moving in harmony. I don't nibble grass, but I walk along at their pace, foraging in my own way, with my eyes picking up small bits of the world around us. Cool enough to stay comfortable in the direct sun and warm enough to stop moving, I have an idea. I'll just sit down. I have another idea. I'll just take off my shoes. And socks. Now my jacket becomes my pillow. The horses come over to investigate. Before long, they have placed me in the center, and they graze around me. It's entirely comforting even though I'm lying on the ground and surrounded by one-thousand-pound animals. I trust them completely. They know exactly where I am and where their feet are. I know this now. I can let go fully.

I close my eyes and feel the ground hold my body. I allow it to support me and release my muscles and joints, all tension slipping away and into the soft dirt. I remember my little girl body in the fields with my dogs. It took decades and so much angst and stress to get back here. Right here. To return to the ground. To be able to relax in my own skin. To be able to stay.

I grew up with The Busy Disease. The pace that was set for me was born a few generations before I was. All over my family tree, there are indicators of a frantic energy that drove all aspects of daily life. Some of it has an adventurous and entrepreneurial spirit running through. There's a go-getter temperament that courses deep on my maternal side. And, on the paternal side, the bloodline goes back to early European explorers. Yet, the frenetic pace has dark underpinnings, a shadow that seems to be running from something in terror. On both sides, there is trauma. Unhealed. Deeply networked and tangled in emotional and relational patterns. Wounds in the family, as well as systemic wounds, religious persecution, immigration, alcoholism and addiction, abuse, and divorce.

The nervous system, in all of its galvanic complexity, has an incredibly basic process when it comes to discerning and responding to threat. We cannot go into analysis paralysis when our lives depend on fight or flight. Single parenting on a meager budget can feel, in the body's pressure system, like trying to outrun a predatory animal. You might not move your legs or respiratory system the same, but vigilance and tenacity become central to even the most benign parts of life. Such was the case for my mother as she trudged through graduate school and pieced together a childhood for me. I observed, learned, and integrated a pace and pressure that became woven into my own system. Already prone to anxiety, my genetic switches flipped on, and a style of fretful functioning became the norm. Internally, the mouse wheel was spinning a mile per minute—so much thinking and obsessing and worrying. Externally, it looked like wild swings of overfunctioning and underfunctioning, a pattern that feeds itself. Exhaustion leads to collapse and then we must race to catch up, only to end up exhausted again. The same pattern played out with all kinds of compulsive behaviors and with my drinking. I worked myself to the bone trying to be good enough, then I drank myself into oblivion trying to unwind.

I managed to achieve, to succeed, to learn things, develop myself, to earn degrees, get jobs, to progress. But it felt like I was doing it with both arms tied behind my back, blindfolded, and holding my breath. Racing to catch up, then falling flat on my face. Along the way, I had a few important animal teachers who came into my life at critical times. My mare, Rosie, was one of them. Only a few weeks sober from alcohol, I decided to shop for a cutting horse. This lineage of Quarter Horses has been bred for their innate instincts to herd cattle, keen minds, strong work ethic, and breathtaking agility. The sports of cutting and reined cow horse are dynamic and incredibly fast-paced. It makes perfect sense that I would find an adrenaline-infused sport while in the middle of a life crisis. If I couldn't change the way I felt with alcohol, I could certainly do so with a fancy horse who loved to chase cows. Before long, I had found this zippy little mare, started riding with an intense trainer, and I was logging at least thirty hours per week in the saddle. In a matter of three months, I had worn all the way through the leather soles of my boots; my socks were hitting my stirrups. I pursued riding and training like my life depended on it.

The thing about working with cows is that there are times when you really do have to hustle. The horse might need to haul down the fence to stop a cow and they give it everything they have. I loved that part. And I loved that Rosie had so much speed and agility. She could turn on a dime and she had a mind that worked like mine. We were like Border Collies. Or Ferrari sports cars. We were high-performance engines who found ourselves redlining. Rosie's natural alertness and instinct made her prone to anxiety too. When her pressure increased, so did her speed. The two of us could unravel together easily, feeding off each other's energy. And we did. Often.

My horse trainer had a tendency to push his students, and it only made my predicament worse. I just did everything harder and faster, and Rosie mirrored my efforts every step of the way. At times, I feared that her legs were going so fast she would just trip over herself. Looking back, that fear was reasonable. It's not safe for mammals, especially prey animals, to be operating at maximum capacity, using all energy and momentum for extended periods unless they are running for their lives. I had threadbare jeans and thin-soled boots, and Rosie was wearing through horseshoes faster than a typical shoeing cycle. But we kept going.

One day we were working cows in the arena. I had been galloping Rosie in circles with what I thought was an effort to warm up. Looking back, I think we were just burning off nervous energy, a habit we had formed after months of our dysregulated pattern. Neither of our minds found calm. We might have been tired, but we were not present. I took Rosie into the herd and began to mull about, eyeing the steer and deciding which one to cut out. It seemed like any other time we had done this. It felt fine.

"Stop. Just stop!" my trainer shouted.

I stopped Rosie and asked, "What's wrong?"

"You're still not stopped!" He yelled through the wind.

"Yes, I am!" I snapped back. I was confused and a bit frustrated.

"Stop riding. Do you even know how to stop riding?" He asked me.

I had no clue what he was trying to tell me. In fact, I was sure that his words were warbled from the windy afternoon, and I was just not hearing him right. I looked around and was trying to see if something was happening around me or if he was talking to someone else. He trotted his horse over to me, a look of astonishment all over his face.

"You stopped your horse. But your whole body kept going. You wiggle. Your hands keep moving. Your eyes are still going. This is why she keeps shifting around and can't settle," he explained.

I listened. I looked down. I could see it and I could feel it. Rosie had stopped and we weren't going forward, but both of us were still moving. It was like we were running in place. I felt my face heat up and the back of my neck tingle. Tears were brewing. "I need a break," I said.

"That's a good idea," he said, "Take a break and walk around. Slowly. Your hands should be soothing your horse. Find a spot to stop. Drop your reins. And stay put. Just stand there."

I didn't know how to stop. I didn't even know how to slow down. I only knew how to collapse, even when I got pregnant and felt the pull of my body, downshifting into a baby-growing pace. I had been working on attending to my needs and changing the ways I lived and cared for myself; however, I was still stricken with The Busy Disease. The residue of overachieving still lingered. I pushed through all signals to slow down. It wasn't until I had a massive ankle sprain that I finally found a speed that my body needed. Or rather, it found me.

That day on Rosie I found a spot to slow down and stop. I found a new location inside of myself, one I had been running from. We rode along the fence line until we both slowed and paused. I took a long breath. So did Rosie. She stopped on her own. I released all of the movement and tension in my limbs, dropped the stirrups and reins, and we stood there. For a long time. We watched other riders. We watched cows. We watched birds. I noticed Rosie's eyelids get heavy and her head dropped a few feet closer to the ground. I put my hand on her neck and she let out the deepest breath I had ever experienced from her.

Eventually, the intense riding and the cow work we had been doing stopped making sense. It wasn't that working cows was altogether wrong for me and Rosie, but we had to find a new rhythm in our relationship, and we needed to do more living and less training. We transitioned our relationship home to our quiet ranch and into pasture life, herd life—the space where we could both find our natural pace. There's no doubt Rosie covers more ground than the rest of her herd. So do I. I'm a fast walker, fast thinker, and I have creative energy that never quits. Rosie is very much the same. But the symptoms of The Busy Disease have mostly passed.

I walk along with the herd as they graze every day. I've been doing this for years, slowly rewiring my muscles and my nervous system. I call it Pasture Time, and I find myself needing it a couple times per day. When I exit the human world and walk through the gate, I enter their world and I'm met with the steady energy of the herd. Maybe it's their giant hearts and heavy bodies. Maybe it's their soulful eyes. Maybe it's their collective commitment to each other and to me. My body downshifts and I can feel a delicious traction and presence return. I don't feel numb or exhausted. I click into the gear that is most authentic to me, my natural pace. I drop into a state of being I've come to love.

The Concept: The Dilemma of Being Awake

Humans have a natural sense of how to adjust pace according to what is needed at any given moment. Adjusting to pace is an ancient instinct and part of our innate capacities to care for ourselves and function in our social groups. All mammals are energy conservers. So, part of our survival systems are hardwired to a "calories in and energy out" formula that allows our engines to run and to have backup energy when needed. Mammals conserve energy and use it appropriately regardless of where they are in the food chain. Predatory mammals conserve energy in case they need extra for fight or flight, or a big boost to take advantage of a hunting opportunity if it presents itself. Prey animals conserve energy so they can spend long hours foraging for food and backup energy for fleeing the scene of dangerous situations.

Mammals have an internal accelerator that signals to us to speed up, slow down, or stop. That sense is an ineffable recognition, instinct-based, and lives in the physical experience of the mammal body. Our nervous systems, using pressure as a signal, communicate to us about pace so that we know when to speed up, slow down, or maintain.

So, what happened to the human animal?

Why are we slow or at a dead stop when we truly need to be quick to respond?

Why do we run full throttle for no good reason?

Remember, we have a brain glitch. The mammal part of our brain has a feel for our natural pace, but the thinking part of our brain overrides it. Essentially, our thoughts and stories drown out our instinct messages. This can happen when our beliefs about performance and achievement increase our speed. Or it can happen when our worries about conflict or our procrastination slow us down. Either way, our bodies try their best to tell us to adjust pace, but we have been socialized and habituated to ignore them.

Some Examples of a Too-Slow Pace

- A manager spends six months watching tense and hostile meetings with an undercurrent of disrespect and fighting polluting the team.
- Changes are underway in a professional organization creating an environment of uncertainty and confusion. The

leadership team waits six weeks to send a company-wide communication about the change process.

- A child is fussy, whiny, and has difficulty following directions. The parent is overwhelmed when the child has a full-blown tantrum a few minutes later.
- A wife says something hurtful to her husband and it takes him days or weeks to let her know. Meanwhile, the pain festers into resentment and affects how he feels and acts.

Some Examples of a Too-Fast Pace

- A new manager starts on the team and is given a huge amount of tactical work with deadlines but without any culture or relationship onboarding. She steps on everyone's toes trying to get the job done without knowing the group dynamics.
- A child is learning to walk, and the parents jump in every time she is about to fall. This slows down her natural learning process and gets in the way of her resilience building.
- During the first week of school, a teacher begins drilling his students, assigning intense work, putting them on the spot in class, and diving into difficult topics. The students are not acclimated to the group culture and never establish psychological safety with the teacher.
- A family rushes through the afternoon and evening so the kids can do extracurricular activities, complete homework, and eat dinner. There is no time for simple connection and presence.

PROBLEMS OF PACE FOR THE HUMAN ANIMAL

WHEN OUR PACE IS TOO SLOW	WHEN OUR PACE IS TOO FAST
We lose momentum or we never get started because we are waiting for all of the perfect pieces to be in place.	Our momentum is not sustainable and we miss signs and signals in the system.
We miss the openings to respond to things or adjust because we are too slow or delayed.	We miss noticing what is needed or we don't choose wisely what to respond to if we are doing too many things at once or moving too quickly.
We can't get a "feel" in the relationship if we never get started.	We can't get a "feel" in the relationship if we are rushing past it.
Creates a build up of pressure or tension that results in numbness, boredom, disengagement, unpredictable explosions, resentment, and blockages.	Creates a build up of pressure or tension that results in overwhelm, flooding, anxiety, accidents, resentment, mistrust, and pain.
We over-assess and end up in "analysis paralysis."	We don't have an opportunity to assess because we are moving too quickly.
We wait too long to respond or shape relationships or situations and then we end up in crisis, reactive, and our approach with others damages trust.	We don't wait long enough for patterns to emerge or for things to adjust or settle naturally so we end up micromanaging which damages trust.

Ease vs. Disease

Returning to the idea that equilibrium is the state of being we are inclined to seek, both in our internal physiological systems and in our relational or environmental systems, homeostasis is the tendency of all living things to move toward balance. Sustainability is key when it comes to pace, so ease is our most optimal state, allowing us to move forward and carry on at a regular pace and without negatively affecting our health. The word "disease" suggests that when we lose our capacity to maintain ease, our physical or mental health is affected. Studying animal groups with the freedom to express their most natural instincts allows us to observe the maintenance of functional pace or those behaviors which allows us to remain functional.

Natural consequences of not attending to pace:
- Exhaustion and overwhelm
- Stress symptoms and patterns
- Anxiety and depression
- Missing the details
- Not attending to relationship
- No time for meaning-making and fulfillment
- Lack of connection or damage in relationships
- Rushing into action doesn't allow us to use scope or see context
- Eroding trust in leadership scenarios
- Emotional reactivity
- Emergencies and crises from delay in responding to signs and symptoms

Grazing and the Calm Alert State

Though we aren't horses, and we don't graze twenty hours per day, we are herd animals, and our mammal bodies are designed to operate in a state of ease, moving in a *calm alert* state as we take care of our daily needs and interact with others. As soon as we layer our modern-day functioning on top of that basic flow, we seem to lose all connection with ease. Instead of finding and maintaining a natural pace, we move back and forth between hyperarousal or stress, and hypoarousal and numbness. Those wild swings have a huge impact on our health and our ability to take care of our relationships.

STATES OF ALERTNESS

HIGH ALERT	CALM ALERT	LOW ALERT
HYPERAROUSED LIVING	**AWARE LIVING**	**NUMB LIVING**
• Life/death situations	• Community and connection	• Busy living
• Constant awareness of life's fragility	• Emotional support	• Overscheduling
• Interrupted sleep	• Safe places for honest sharing	• Drugs and alcohol
• Intense schedule	• Nourishing activities/Rest	• Sleeping too much
• Away from home	• Interdependent relationships for shared awareness	• Overeating or unhealthy eating
• Physical stress	• Tools for managing stress and feelings	• Isolation and avoidance
• Physical trauma	• Processes for coping with your life	• Silence about stress
• Emotional trauma	• Spiritual practice	• Compulsive activities like working out, gaming, shopping, electronic devices
• Witness to trauma	• Care of your body	• Television
• Emotional fatigue	• Time outdoors	• Stuffing pain
• Overstimulated nervous system	• Meaningful conversation	• Boredom
• Intense pace	• Mentorship and guidance	• Codependent living/ Focusing on others
• Self-defense	• Emotional intimacy	• Limited emotional availability
• Hypervigilance	• Presence and gratitude in everyday life	
• Reliance on instincts	• Noticing details and beauty	
• Necessity to be reactive	• People who know you and see you	**DANGER**
• Constant sense of danger	• Accountability system that keeps you honest	• Fatigue
DANGER	• Opportunities to be of service to others	• Weight issues
		• Depression
• Fatigue	**SAFETY**	• Anger/Irritability
• GI symptoms		• Heart problems
• Anxiety/Depression/Panic	• Rested	• Blood pressure
• Anger/Irritability	• Stable mood	• Chronic pain
• Insomnia	• Normal aches and pains	
• Chronic pain	• Generally peaceful	

Pace in Our Relationships

Humans think, feel, process, and integrate at different rates. There is no "right" pace. A healthy group (human or other animal) allows for varying paces in order to stay in close enough proximity to share resources like awareness, protection, warmth, and food. We have the capability to modulate ever so slightly to accommodate the wide range. We get into trouble when we create a hierarchy of pace in our group culture, leading to unnecessary competition and fear. Because our current human culture values accomplishment and productivity, speed has the prestige. This makes it particularly challenging to find our natural pace. We are often ignoring our internal rhythms to match the external ones, and we have become numb or lack awareness altogether. Spend an hour or an afternoon grazing with a horse herd and you can learn a whole lot of lessons about pace. To most humans, the equine grazing pace seems like a standstill; however, the herd is almost always moving.

Human animals carry an underlying fear that if we slow down our interactions, we will break connection, the silence will be awkward, or we will be judged harshly for not keeping up or for underperforming. We have layers of self-judgment and external pressures signaling us to go faster. We succumb to those pressures until exhaustion so that we aren't able to be appropriately responsive or reactive when we need to act or relate more quickly. It's quite a conundrum!

How to Attend to Pace and Find Ease

If you listen to others' conversations, you'll find that people leave very little time to pause, breathe, or think before they speak and respond. If you observe interactions and study movement, you can see that humans are often misaligned with the rhythm or pace of what is needed for the circumstances. The bottom line is this: If we aren't paying attention, our belief systems, cultural expectations, and lifestyle habits influence our pace and interfere with our natural sense of what is needed to find more balance.

Relationships have a natural pace, and if we pay attention to our internal signals, we can adjust so the relationship can find a pace that is sustainable and encourages safety, trust, compatibility, and flow.

Here are some tips that can help you develop more fluency with your pace:

- Check in with yourself and others by asking directly about pace.
- Request to others if you need more time or if you need things to move faster.
- Experiment with making decisions to see if you act in haste or if there's too much drag in your process.
- Try to slow down first so that you can choose the appropriate pace rather than it choosing you.
- Notice pace in your body signals and identify how it affects sensations like pressure, tension, stress, apathy, or boredom.
- Target different times of the day or vary your normal activities so that you can practice different paces to find what feels natural or optimal.
- Observe how people respond to you when you slow down your speech and allow for more space in conversations, or what happens when you speed things up.

- Notice times of your day that are particularly harried or chaotic and try slowing down to see if you are more efficient and can use less of your time by going slower.
- Consider any major areas of life like career, education, or relationship and ask if the pace with which you are engaged matches your needs or if you need to adjust in a way that is more suitable for you.
- When you feel compelled to shift your pace, pause and ask yourself if it's necessary or if you are being guided by self-judgement or fear of others' judgment.

The Practice: Finding Your Natural Pace

Our daily or weekly schedules are great sources of data for our problems with pace. We might think that we are at an optimal pace, but without studying it and tuning in to our mammal bodies, it is often our thinking brain making those assessments. As always, we want to look at things with our rational mind, but Natural Leadership asks us to bring the animal part of us into focus so that we have a full picture.

Part One: Too Fast

First, you are going to identify how your pace might be too fast. Take a look at your weekly calendar and identify a day of the week that is most stressful for you. Now, as you look at that day, find the time of day that is most hectic and when you are moving the fastest. You've isolated a great time period during which to study pace and "feel" in yourself and your relationships. As you approach that day/time, do so with your scientific hat. Use your newfound tool of *scope* and see if you can zoom out in order to really study yourself.

1. What do you notice in your body as you slow down? Are you more relaxed or do you have agitation or restlessness? Do some writing about what might be contributing to this.

2. As you slow down, what do you notice in your relationships with others? Does it make good sense for you to speed through the experience? Is it possible you are running from something to avoid discomfort or anxiety?

3. Do some writing about the "feel" or the "give/take" that is possible when you slow down and attend to pace and relationship. Is there more communication occurring than you realized?

4. Look for a moment when you can pretend to do a slow-motion video. You are going to move yourself (body and mind) through the moment like molasses. What do you notice in yourself? In others?

Part Two: Too Slow

Again, look at your calendar for the week. This time, study the places in your routine when you are too slow. Identify an activity (work, home, school, kids, partner) when you typically feel irritable. As you approach that activity, study yourself and others. Look for moments when you are slow to respond to your needs or when your feedback to others is nonexistent. Study what happens to you in these situations.

1. Are you unaware of your slow pace or are you editing yourself and choosing not to shape your experience?

2. Is the delay in your leadership about fear of judgment or fear of hurting others?

3. Experiment with increasing your response time, even if you do it clumsily, and what do you notice in how others react? How does it feel in your body when you respond more quickly? Does it give you more energy or less energy?

You can do this practice as often as you need in order to get a feel for your natural pace. Remember that pace is habituated and our bodies develop patterns that we are not aware of. As you use your Natural Leadership Awareness and focus on this concept of pace, you will begin to find a calm alert state, also known as ease. You'll know when you find it. And you'll likely want more of it!

CHAPTER SIX

Feel

If we want to support each other's inner lives, we must remember a simple truth: the human soul does not want to be fixed, it wants simply to be seen and heard.

PARKER PALMER

There is a voice that doesn't use words. Listen.

RUMI

We no longer plow the land together; today we talk. We have come to glorify verbal communication. I speak; therefore I am. We naively believe that the essence of who we are is most accurately conveyed through words.

ESTHER PEREL

The Story: How the Body Whispers

The assignment was to put a notebook and a pen by the bedside and to go to sleep with the hope of both dreaming and recollecting the dream. It was 2002, and I was getting my graduate degree in counseling psychology with the intention of becoming a therapist.

It was such a joy that it seemed almost laughable to get to study Jungian theory and dream analysis as part of my professional path. I had always been fascinated by dream symbolism and the many layers of the human conscious and unconscious worlds. The ten-week course in dreamwork allowed a surface exploration of psychiatrist Carl Jung's writings. And the real exciting part was the experiential assignment, which asked us to take a deep dive into one or two dreams and to study and write about them.

I followed the instructions and approached my sleep preparation with great care. Always a prolific dreamer, I had no doubt I'd have vivid memories of my dreams. Sure enough, I was waking each morning with detailed narratives, rich imagery, and emotional material, all readily available for me to scribble into my notebook. Our professor asked us to keep it up and to look for a dream that asked for attention. He taught us about the concept of the "big dream." Big dreams carry powerful lessons and wake-up calls, and often they are so powerful, the dreamer will recall them for the rest of their life. Jung wrote, "Who looks outside, dreams; who looks inside, awakes." Not all of us would have a big dream, but I really wanted one.

After a few days, I woke up with the big dream right there, as if it were stamped between my eyes or lingering on my tongue. The main character was a beautiful bay mare who was lost and wandering a valley. Riva came to me in that dream. I studied and garnered all of the messages from that visit during my class and my writing. Twenty years later, she came to me again. This time she appeared in a very real physical form, a stray horse walking down the road in our town. She was picked up by the county animal control and then spent two weeks at the shelter. Though the shelter mostly deals with dogs and cats, we're in a rural area, so it's not unusual for animal control to handle livestock at times.

When no one claimed the mare, two women who ran a dog rescue sprung her from the shelter and took her home to foster her. The mare stayed there for a few months, and it was with those women that she was given her name. They thought they'd keep her for a while, but Riva shuffled around a bit until landing with my friend Tami. When I met Riva and heard her story, my big dream came back to me. I wasn't looking to add any horses to my herd at that time, but Riva appeared. I had the sense that she should come home with me, at least for a bit. As I led her toward my trailer, I saw the muscles along her hips quiver, her eyes widen. I took a hold of the lead rope, and I could feel her take a hold too. She braced. She began to tell her story.

For the first few days she was here, I did very little with Riva. I just let her settle and orient to the ranch, check out the other horses, and get a sense of me. I decided to move her into a corral where she could start socializing with the herd. I put a halter on her and stroked her neck. I remembered what she communicated at the trailer, so I went slow and waited. We breathed together. Then I picked up the lead rope with the gentlest touch. She threw her head and shook it violently like her face was under attack. *Aha! There's part of her story.* I didn't know what happened, what went right or wrong, but she showed me that she had a sensitivity. And I listened.

We had that same conversation for about four weeks. Each time I led her and with each point of contact, she showed me who she was as an individual and her sensitivity to touch and to pressure. She told me, with her flapping head, that she wanted me to know this about her and she wanted me to take it seriously. So I did. I listened and I responded. I lightened my hand as much as I could, which told her, "I hear you. I see you." I breathed. I waited. I had love in my heart and patience in my body. And then we moved on.

With each activity we did together, she would show me another layer of herself. She had stories to tell about brushing, saddling, bridling, riding, trotting, bathing, feeding. Pretty much any place where humans may have intersected with her world, her body, her being. By quietly waiting, paying attention, and listening, she revealed some baggage. This girl had a lot to say! And the more willingness and patience I showed her, the more her connection, affection, and willingness to partner returned.

She wasn't a wild animal or an unhandled horse when I met her; however, there were all of these ways she acted like it. The essence of her, the most authentic part of her survival system, was on high alert. Instead of learning to open and bond, she had learned to guard. There was a physical space and a register of time I needed to learn in order to sync up with Riva. It started within me. I had to gather my inner world and soften. I had to lead with a completely clear channel of energy in my mind, body, and emotions. If I started there and waited, I could feel when Riva was ready to enter the space between us. In the theories and methods of natural horsemanship, this is often referred to as *the soft feel*, and it is something we can create with our horses if we can prepare ourselves to connect and we can learn to wait. Legendary horseman Tom Dorrence wrote about this in his book, *True Unity*, "The true unity and willing communication between the horse and me is not something that can be handed to someone, it has to be learned, it has to come from the inside of a person and inside of the horse."

Many horse people approach training from that old paradigm of "breaking" these animals, relating through intimidation, pain, and control. The relationships are based in fear, not in trusting partnership. For thousands of years, humans have taken the horse's very unique way of being in the world and interfered. Horses have a finely tuned system of communicating and collaborating, a sensitive feedback system with which they conduct their relationships. The herd has cultural rules each member knows in their cells. For generations, humans have willfully tried to break this. Fortunately, in the last sixty to seventy-five years, the tide has changed in the horse world. A small but growing segment of the horse community started to study indigenous horsemanship around the world and began to see that the horse's way, the language of Equus, had something to teach us. Some people refer to it as *horse whispering*, which is actually quite accurate. Humans have to be willing to shut our mouths, to put aside our stubbornness and or egos, and to listen and learn from the horses. We have to be willing to communicate in their language. It's quiet—like a whisper—but if you open your eyes and your heart, the horses have so much to teach us.

Just like the misattuned treatment of horses, people are often "trained" in a similar fashion. We're raised, taught, managed, and married in ways that betray the soft feel between mammals. Some of us are or were handled roughly, either physically, emotionally, or both. It may not be exactly like the old cowboy way, but humans do have a way of crashing through that sacred space between each other instead of learning to wait and listen. We each have a tenderness, a near perfect sensitivity that we are hardwired to protect, and when it is handled brutishly, we shut down. We brace and guard ourselves just like Riva. Too often, and with complete ignorance, we plow through each other's sensitivities like heavy machinery. The sad thing is that those beautiful human instincts are just right, exquisitely designed, and that reckless way of relating really does break something within us.

The Concept: Creating Feel in Relationship

Relationships exist in the space between us. Between two beings of any species, there is relational potential. We can call that *feel*. When we begin to operate with feel, we leave enough room for others to reach for the relationship, which means that there is a natural draw or desire to connect. A great deal is communicated if we can wait, watch, and notice. If we slow down and use pace, we can feel much more. Too often, humans crash into that space and insist on relationship and contact. Because of our social agreement to ignore our own needs and be polite, we learn to live with this affront though it impinges and creates pressure in our bodies. The invisible, or barely visible, space between us is where we navigate and negotiate. It's where we begin to grow trust and learn about each other. It takes time, and it takes the use of other Natural Leadership elements such as awareness, scope, and pace in order to decipher and utilize all that occurs in that space. At the heart of what we create when we feel is a deep listening and respect for another being's inner world. We make ourselves available and wait for the other person (or animal) to seek connection, to feel safe enough to soften, and to want it. When we look at connection and trust on these terms, the micromoments when we move toward each other are sacred. One of the most respected teachers and trainers of horsemanship, Ray Hunt, said about this, "There's a spot in there, inside the horse, an opening where there is no fear or resistance, and that's what I began looking for." We can take this exact practice and apply it to our human relationships. We can look for that opening and know that we are building relationships of pure trust.

We have to earn the right to ask for something. We earn it by offering to be a partner in shared awareness and by taking the time to create feel. This allows us to better understand how another person experiences the world. Operating from a feel in the relationship is about using all of our Natural Leadership senses, truly tapping into our mammalian signals so that we can feel ourselves and attune with another being. When we use feel, others will naturally seek connection. We will feel another reach for the relationship. Some people call this attraction, charisma, leadership, or presence.

The Benefits of Creating Feel in Relationships

When we attune to others and are genuinely curious about who they are, we show others that we are:

- Committed to learning how they operate and what matters to them
- Willing to pay attention to their preferences and sensitivities
- Eager to get along
- Interested in building trust
- Desiring connection and shared experiences
- Willing to adapt and adjust in order to create a relational flow

Draw and Drive

All mammals' relationships exist in a constant state of tension, seeking balance between our needs for autonomy and our needs for connection. The concepts of draw and drive are opposing yet interconnected forces or pressures that affect all mammals and primarily have to do with how we adjust to emotional and physical proximity in order to maintain relationships and maintain our ability to take care of ourselves as individuals. Draw and drive exist internally, in our relational systems, and in our environment. When we work with feel, we notice the elements of draw and drive in ourselves and in others. This awareness allows us to use draw and drive as natural motivators.

What are the elements of draw in the illustration?
- The carriage is being pulled.
- The barn likely creates some natural draw for the animal to want to head home.
- The grass on the side of the road might create some draw as the animal gets hungry.

What are the elements of drive in the illustration?
- Once the carriage gets moving, it puts a bit of pressure on the animal's hind end.
- The human driver of the carriage uses his voice, energy, reins, and whip to motivate the animal forward.
- Anything surprising in the environment could create some pressure to move away or move faster.

Natural Draw

Draw is an energy or an internal sense that pulls us in a specific direction. All mammals, including humans, have sensitivity to draw. It is an attraction to something we want or need. It can be triggered by instinct, survival, intuition, body, emotions, curiosity, creativity, or attachment. We can be drawn toward freedom or drawn toward connection. Draw is a natural phenomenon occurring within and around us and we can become skilled at noticing when it is occurring and how to work with it. When we learn to feel the draw in relationships, we can make adjustments to attend to our needs or to the needs of others.

Relationships without enough draw:

- Don't inspire us
- Don't feel welcoming
- Are often lacking warmth or affection

Relationships with too much draw:

- Make it hard for us to be ourselves
- Feel smothering and confusing
- Create a sense of panic, urgency, or emergency

Natural Drive

Drive is a pressure or energy that creates movement and/or space. It is used when a push is needed. Just like draw, drive is a fundamental part of all mammals' experience in relationship to each other and to their environments. We use drive to set direction, create boundaries, ask for space, and inspire motion.

Relationships without enough drive:

- Lack clarity and direction
- Don't feel safe
- Create anxiety

- Feel limp and lifeless

Relationships with too much drive:

- Are exhausting
- Create stress
- Don't allow for enough freedom

Preparing to Work with Feel

These are some questions that can help you prepare yourself to work with feel. Remember, feel begins within you.

- Have you checked in with your mind, emotions, and body so that you have a soft and willing feel inside of you?
- Have you checked your motives or agendas to be sure that you are leading with clean energy rather than emotionally reactive or confusing energy?
- Are you moving freely in your body, and do you have an attitude of openness?
- Are you tapping into a sense of desire and intention that is free of fear, expectations, story, disappointments, or force?
- Are you listening to the internal state of the other being?
- Are you visualizing and imagining what you want to create in the relationship?
- Are you being intentional and sensitive as you use influence and pressure?
- Do you have access to a vulnerable and open part of yourself and your heart?

How to be a Human Whisperer

You can become a human whisperer with just a slight pivot. You can approach others with some simple but profoundly effective shifts:

1. Assume there is a story. Everyone has a story, good or bad. Be prepared to look for it so that you can get to know what others have walked through and who they are.
2. Lighten your touch. Horses love the soft feel of our hands. It turns out people don't like it if you knock down the door of their spirit and come crashing in. In this age of vulnerability, we have gotten a bit pushy about sharing and digging into each other's inner worlds. We need to respect, honor, and learn how to soften and slow down our approach in relationships so that trust can be built naturally. It can't be forced.
3. Keep a curious mindset. Listening carefully and observing goes a long way. But when we take personally what we see, or take too much responsibility for another's stories, we can no longer see them accurately. It's called projection, and it's a huge problem for humans. Allowing others to have a separate but relevant experience in the world without inserting ourselves is one of the kindest relational moves we can make. Use your empathy muscles without allowing your own feelings or stories to dominate you as a listener. Empathy without projection is a clear channel of compassion.
4. Be patient. People may need to show you or tell you their story many times. Making meaning of our experiences is unique to our human mind, and it's how we process who we are. It's how we learn and how we heal. Listening with-

out judgment and without trying to fix allows others to feel seen without feeling broken.

5. Slow down and be quiet. It's simply impossible to increase our awareness of ourselves or our relationships if we are too busy, allowing too much noise or stimulation into our lives, or moving too quickly. Horses are great role models for setting a wise pace. They graze for twenty hours per day. It's a slow and steady and peaceful progression through the world. If you watched a movie of your life, you would want to cry at how fast your pace is. Most people are shocked when they finally do slow down. Our worlds are full of amazing moments all day long. And, when we change our pace, we're able to experience those moments, have a deeper connection to ourselves, and be much more available to relate more intentionally with the world of living things around us.

The Practice: Listening for the One Question

When humans are interacting, we communicate too quickly and often get caught up in the momentum of our social interplay. We listen but all the while we are thinking about ourselves, about the next thing we are going to say, or what question we might want to ask. We get out ahead of ourselves, and then we are unable to attune to others. It's a bit like running too fast down a hill. Gravity gets the best of us, and we fall on our faces.

We want to look for opportunities to slow down so we can build a larger space for feel in our relationships. When we listen and wait, we become more attuned to timing and to natural openings when the other person is ready for more relationship. This is a nonverbal skill, and we actually need to release ourselves of the pressure of language and of overthinking so we can read the signals that have much more to do with our inner worlds.

You are going to look for a listening opportunity during which you stay mostly quiet other than practicing presence and active listening. You are going to avoid interfering with the other person and instead give them space and time to talk.

You can practice this with anyone in your life. Here are a few examples of scenarios that can work well for this:

- Your child is struggling with a friendship issue.
- A colleague has had a conflict with their boss.
- A client has had a really challenging and painful week.
- Your friend has been fighting with their romantic partner.

How to Listen
- Focus on the emotional process and feel instead of the narrative content, details, and facts.
- Listen for the "heart of the matter."
- Hold back your impulse to find solutions or fix feelings.
- Notice your ego-making noise in the background and listen past the self-chatter.
- Listen with your imagination and allow your mind to drift into reverie. Notice if images come to mind or any daydream-like content emerges.
- As you listen, notice moments when your body feels tension or pressure and you are likely close to the heart of the issue.

Purpose of This Technique
- It slows us down and asks us to wait until the most important and meaningful question emerges.

- A slower process allows us to keep our scope and see the big picture and context of what we are hearing.
- While we wait for the question to emerge, we can tune into pressure, which might give us important information about ourselves or the other person.

By waiting and seeking the one question, you are practicing moderation, intentionality, consciousness, scope, pace, and the feel of relationship. If you wait long enough and keep yourself calm and centered, a question will likely emerge. It helps to pretend that you are only allowed to ask one question. Just wait until that one question comes to you. When you think you've found it, sit with it a bit longer and breathe. Stay tuned in with the other person and see if you can find the moment when they are open to you making contact, when they might be ready for a question. Ask your question and see if the relational space, the feel, can stay soft. If you or the other person starts to get guarded, go back to listening and try again. This is all about practice and learning to develop the skill of listening and waiting.

CHAPTER SEVEN

Power

There is a set of mechanics, invisible to most of us, but consistent in every conversation, whether high stakes or low. These mechanics determine who has control—who leads, who follows, what is under discussion, and where the conversation will go next.

KASIA URBANIAK

Most people do not really want freedom, because freedom involves responsibility, and most people are frightened of responsibility.

SIGMUND FREUD

The Story: Take a Chance

There we were in the sandy arena, one more time, having the same nonverbal conversation about personal space that we had been having for fifteen years. He would push his shoulder into my back, and I'd lose my balance. Or he'd flagrantly disregard the pace of my human legs and hurry past me, wrenching my arm and shoulder as I would cling to the lead rope trying to keep ahold of him.

I'd stroke his white blaze with the finest face brush, and he'd thrust his giant head into my chest. Chance was the equine love of my life, and for many years, I didn't even know our relationship was a problem for me. Perhaps it was so much like my other relationships that I couldn't see it for what it was. Maybe I was too numb to notice or to feel the sting of disrespect. We don't know what we cannot see. And we just don't see it until we're ready.

"Don't let him drag you around like that. Get after him!" Billy said as he shook his head and walked through the gate. I felt a zap of shame, heat running up my neck and into my scalp. Shame lives everywhere, even in our skin. "He drives me crazy. I mean, I love him to death. But he won't stop walking all over me," I said. Billy carried on with his own business, walked off to put a horse away, and then returned with another. He paused to grab a cold drink, then he stood at the fence taking long gulps as he watched me and Chance in our relationship dance. I spun the lead rope and asked Chance to respect my space. He'd move away a bit. Then he'd give me a look and start veering back toward me. I allowed it and could feel the draw toward him. He wanted to be close to me. I felt loved. We took a few steps toward each other, paused for a greeting, and then Chance pushed right through me and stepped on my foot. I swung the lead rope, and the leather popper grazed his shoulder. "Cut it out, Chance!" I shouted at him and felt the anger burning in my throat. I chased him off and kept him moving.

I could feel the added pressure of Billy as he stood there, this perceptive witness who offered very little in the way of words but so much in presence. I knew he had opinions and judgments and suggestions. Why wouldn't he help me? Why was he just standing there watching me struggle? It wasn't the first time I'd asked those questions in my head, blaming others for not helping me even when I hadn't asked for help. And it certainly wouldn't be the last time I felt alone and unrescued in a problem I didn't know how to solve. But a pivotal moment occurred as Billy stood there doing nothing. Through a film of confusion, I became aware that I was at a turning point. I faced a choice I didn't know how to make. I needed to stand my ground and ask him not to crowd me, and I needed to follow through. But something in me kept caving, an inner crumbling.

I dropped the conflict between me and Chance. I dropped the lead rope. I dropped my sense of self, my leadership. I left it all lay- ing in the sandy hoofprints below my feet. Frustrated and blaming Billy, I closed the physical gap between me and my horse that I had worked so hard to create. I went to him for comfort—rushed, like I couldn't get to him quick enough. I leaned into him and stroked his neck. There was an emotional twitch, like a spasm of guilt that wouldn't let up. Maybe I'd been too hard on him. "You're such a good boy, Chancey. Such a good boy." Who was I praising or comforting? What was the offense? Who had been wronged? I was so fused to Chance that I could barely see where he ended and I began. Were we bonded? Sure. But this was more of an entangle- ment than a relationship. It was a web of needs, demands, fears, and longing to be loved, a mess I found myself in often. This horse and I had fallen into a trap from the very beginning.

I met Chance when he was barely three years old. He'd been ridden about a dozen times. I heard about him through a friend and his story pulled at something deep within my emotional world. At the time, I didn't know much about that part of me. It was like an invisible string on my emotional instrument that certain people or situations could reach and play. When the string was played, its unique tune was a song of hardship and tragedy, and it became the only thing I could hear. I was naturally drawn to rescue stories, and if they involved an animal, I was all in.

Chance had been referred to as a rescue horse. So, when I first heard his story, my ears perked up. In truth, he was a runaway horse. As a weanling, he was purchased by a hot mess of a woman who named him Jägermeister, the German digestif to be sipped after big meals. In America, it's often guzzled from shot glasses in fraternity houses and dive bars. The woman kept him in the yard of a motorcycle repair shop owned by her boyfriend. People in the town knew about the junkyard horse and there was a significant hum of concern about his living conditions and the lack of nutrition and companionship. His owner would go away for days at a time and leave him without food and water. People didn't think highly of her or how she was neglecting the horse.

At some point, Chance decided that the broken-down motorcycles were not suitable equine buddies and that there must be something better down the road. He broke out of the junkyard, trotted himself a couple of miles, and made his way into a lush, irrigated pasture where five other horses lived. Though no one really knows what happened that evening, it did appear that he got tangled in the barbed wire trying to get into the pasture. When my friends, Dale and Jo, found him the next morning, he was unconscious with his hind end completely tangled in the wire. His flesh was torn to the bone, and he had lost a lot of blood. They nursed him back to health, told his previous owner to lose their number, and they worked with animal control so they could keep him. After several months of healing and putting weight on him, they started riding him with the intent of finding a new owner for him. And they renamed him Chance because he took a chance on his own life when he left the junkyard and journeyed toward a better existence. He knew his own needs.

When I saw him, I knew that he was going to be my equine partner as I took a chance on an unknown adventure of my own. His story was compelling, his eyes were kind, his heart was giant and right there, ready to connect with mine. I didn't see it then, but his story paralleled my own in many ways—in too many ways. It would take years for me to wake up and begin to see how we intertwined into a gorgeous mess of experiences and lessons. The point where our lives converged made perfect sense to me at the time. I had a bright and shiny poetry degree and no job prospects. I also had an adventurous but slightly frantic urge to buy a horse and move to California. It made perfect sense to me. No one in my life challenged this plan. I was like a stray dog scampering down the road, cars passing all day, and no one stopped to ask if I was lost. I was lost. Very lost. But I didn't really see that. I just knew that I had fallen in love with this young horse whose story captivated me. I needed to gallop through the golden hills of California on his back. I wanted him to carry me somewhere. Anywhere. Into a big, new experience.

We had a major crash during our first month together. It's like we hit rock bottom before our relationship had even started. I certainly wouldn't see it that way. Not until many years later. Only weeks after moving him to a new ranch and with very little experience riding him, I jumped onto him bareback. The details are gruesome and accentuate just how disconnected and garbled my reality had become. I was at a barbecue and getting to know the community of horse people who kept their horses at the ranch. It had been a fun time with food and drinks and laughter. As the sun dipped behind the hills, Cowboy Joe started a bonfire and the bottle of whiskey emptied fast. I don't have much memory, but I do recall walking up a dark hill to find and halter my horse. And I recall propping open the door of a Porta Potty so I could climb onto the sink and launch myself onto his back. I came back to consciousness the next day in the hospital with three skull fractures.

For the next fifteen years, Chance and I had a bipolar partnership. With no stable leadership in our duo, our path was a circuitous one, a confusing mix of beautiful experiences and stormy ones. Power imbalances in relationships are a lot like this with wild swings. Sometimes it felt like trying to open a heavy gate with frozen hinges. Other times, that same gate would slam shut in my face. I had no sense of how to work with it, how to grease up the relationship so that it could flow with more ease. Chance was definitely a heavy gate, better at blocking or controlling movement than creating it. And I was a young woman struggling to find my own feet, more lost than I knew. I could barely lead myself, let alone a horse who needed a consistent partner. I looked to him for so much direction. I looked to him to see myself. I looked to him until I learned to look to myself. I looked to him until I learned to take responsibility for myself.

I didn't know that moment in the arena held so much significance. It was just another power struggle between me and the horse I loved. With no consciousness, I had accepted the extremes of our relational swings as normal. After the drama of our interaction had settled, I saddled Chance and hopped on him. We rode through the vineyards, the quiet rustle of grape leaves surrounding us. Squirrels scurried in and out of their tunnels and crossed the red dirt path as Chance ambled along with heavy steps. He had a very sleepy way about him so much of the time. Billy told me he was dull, and I thought it was an insult, but it was just a very accurate description. It had always been a point of incompatibility between me and Chance. Though the fog of my own life path was thick at times, I had always been a keen observer of my surroundings.

We got back to the barn, and I gave Chance a long bath. I brushed his mane and his thick tail and watched him nibble from the grain bucket as he dried in the late sun. I put him back in his paddock and walked around the corner to get Rosie, the young mare who had become my primary riding horse. As I went to put her halter on, she dropped her head six inches and gently leaned toward me, as if to say, "Here, let me make this easier for you." I took a big breath and let the air seep out, all of the pressure and tension leaving me like the final moments as a balloon loses its shape. We matched our steps as we walked toward the area where Billy was getting his next horse ready to ride. I could feel Rosie on the other end of the lead rope, light and willing. Our relationship dance was different than the one I had with Chance. There was no confusion. Instead, it was a clear conversation, a give and take, a sharing of ideas and suggestions. It was like we played music together. Better yet, it was like we wrote the songs.

"You know, Beth. You'll need to have that conversation with him every time," Billy said.

"Every time?" I asked.

"Yup. Every time. He's not gonna change," Billy said, slowing to a stop and facing me.

"I don't want to."

"Right," he said, as he looked me straight in the eye.

"I don't want to," I repeated.

I finally heard myself. It was the first movement, the smallest step toward letting go. I didn't know if I had let go of the relationship patterns or the whole relationship, but I knew I had changed. I noticed something different inside of me. I had brought a new version of myself to my relationship with Rosie. I liked how I felt, an exquisite mix of freedom and power, of lightness and leverage.

There was a flow in our connection I hadn't known before, and I wanted more of it.

Ours was a tumultuous love story, and I had already written the happily-ever-after ending. I bought my dream ranch and named it after Chance, imagining he would live out his days grazing with friends. I would make coffee and watch him from my kitchen window. Take a Chance Ranch seemed like exactly the right name. But once he was here, he struggled to settle. As more horses came into my herd, Chance seemed to become more agitated. He had always been a friendly horse, the kind of guy who other horses liked to be around. He was eager to make new friends. Something had changed. On two occasions, he attacked and injured other horses who had done nothing to provoke him. To protect the rest of my horses, I kept him separate. Then I moved him to a friend's place to see if he could settle there. And he did.

For several months, Chance lived on the other side of town and with another herd. It was hard for me at first. Stuck in the narrative of our shared life together, I couldn't let go of angst. The plot had twisted in a way I hadn't written. When I went to visit him, something seemed different. There was a faraway look in his eyes and a flatness to our connection. I wondered if I had unplugged or if he had. Either way, there was barely a current between us. We weren't looking to each other for much relationship. The spark was gone.

On a hot afternoon in June, Chance had a grand mal seizure. When he came out of it, the light in his eyes was dimmer. His heart seemed counties away. It was like the horse I knew and loved wasn't there. I wondered out loud if his behavior changes and the seizure pointed to some kind of a brain growth. The vet agreed that this was likely but at his advanced age it made no sense to start doing any diagnostic work. It was possible that he could live peacefully and not have any more seizures, so I decided to give that a go. But I needed to find a more permanent living situation for him, and I knew he couldn't come home with me and risk disrupting my peaceful herd.

The day Chance left, I slowed myself down so I could feel along the way. I gave him a good bath and groomed him. I ran my fingers along his hips and his back, noticing how his shape had changed with age—the bones more pronounced, his spine more swayed. I walked along with him as he grazed. I recalled all our years together and the ways I had grown. There were core lessons about my own personal power that I would not have learned if it weren't for Chance. He was exactly the teacher I needed.

I struggled to accept that I wouldn't be able to practice my new relational skills with him. I wanted our relationship to be transformed and resolved. I wanted our story to have a tidy ending. In some ways, it did. I loaded him onto the trailer headed to a retirement pasture a couple of hours south. The hinges squeaked and the steel door echoed as Chance's hind end disappeared. The diesel engine roared to life, and the rig crept along the dirt road as they headed to the gate. I paused for a moment and then began to walk away. Chance went one way, and I went the other. It was a goodbye. An ending. A resolution. We would each carry on. Just not together.

The Concept: The Relational Gates

Power. Control. We read the words. They pull us in. At the same time as we're enticed, we also bristle and balk. We have a love–hate relationship with the topics of power and control, mostly because we don't fully understand them. We associate power with the misuse or abuse of it. We imagine people who overpower or rule or dictate. When we think of power, we are often considering one extreme end of the spectrum, a power that causes pain, fear, and damage to our relationships. Control has an equally bad reputation. Who wants to be called a control freak or a micromanager? When we think of control, we think of someone who runs a tight ship with a lot of rules and rigidity. Or we think of a person who prevents others from doing what they want. The inflammatory nature of these associations gets in our way of understanding the underlying nature of the phenomenon of power and control.

Defining Power and Control

Let's start with some definitions of power and control that can help to neutralize things a bit. Power is defined as the ability to influence. It's the gas pedal. To influence others and our surroundings, we use all parts of ourselves: body language, words, tone, eye contact, emotions, voice, energy. In the world of mammals, power is the energy and communication that moves things forward and is a necessary part of all aspects of life. Control is defined as the ability or capacity to modulate or adjust influence. It's the brake pedal. We modulate elements of power in our environment by giving feedback to others. We allow influence in by inviting it or we don't allow it in by blocking it. Humans, and all other animals, use power and control in order to take care of themselves, care for others, negotiate needs, share resources, and navigate changes in the environment.

We express power and exercise control in many different ways. Our body language and the energy with which we relate is full of communication. We can muscle others with our tone or facial expressions, or we can block and resist in total silence. Pay attention to interactions going on around you and look for the dance of power and control at play. It's a perfectly natural phenomenon in all mammal relationships. It happens within us, between us, and all around us. The problem is that we do not necessarily learn about or become skilled at utilizing this natural element of our mammal system. Like most of our natural capacities, if we are using them, they are using us. This isn't a big deal when power and control are in balance. Remember, homeostasis is what we are striving for. However, it's an all-too-common problem in our human relationships to have power and control swinging wildly, along with our relational and emotional stability.

Examples of Power and Control in Balance

Let's start with what it looks like when power and control have a flow and when the relational gates are operating well. Things are low conflict and well-regulated.

Here are some examples:

- I share these ideas (power) and you consider them (control).
- You ask your child to help clear the table (power), and she lifts her plate with a smile (control).
- You tell your boss you'd like a raise (power), and she agrees to consider your request (control).
- You offer advice to a friend (power), and he listens (control).
- Your sister shares a story (power) from her heart, and you feel inspired (control).
- A horse pins her ears and asks for space (power), and the other horse moves out of the way (control).

One person attempts to influence, and the other person allows for the influence. It can be a beautiful dance, especially when a relationship has been built on trust and mutual influence and those dynamics have been practiced. We can take turns being in the influence position. In fact, a position of power carries with it immense responsibility, and all mammals need a break from that. Sharing power allows one mammal to hold space for others so their nervous systems can drop some or all awareness and rest, in a similar way as they share awareness.

We all know that power often feels out of whack, off-kilter, and full of tension or resistance. We ask for something, and we get a brick wall in return. Others reject our influence in overt and subtle ways. We sit there, perplexed, saddened that we simply cannot make life happen. Power becomes confusing and frustrating, and relationships take on dead-end patterns that are repetitive and corrosive. Think of your influence as a power cord. It has no juice unless it's plugged in to the wall and the electricity is flowing.

Genuine Power Is an Energy Inside of Us

Genuine and balanced power is not about making others do things. It isn't about compliance—yours or anyone else's. It is about influencing from an internal place so alive and vibrant that those around you deeply want to go along with your requests, to be part of your vision, and to join or match the excited and inspired energy you are putting out into the world. We have to be willing to go out on a limb and allow others to see, hear, and feel what we envision. And, as importantly, we have to be willing to hold space for others to see and hear and feel what is happening inside of them. We have no influence without earning it, and care and presence with others is the primary way we achieve that.

Where does our influence go wrong? Maybe we doubt ourselves or question the legitimacy of our ask. Perhaps we've been sitting on our request and feeling self-pity or resentment for a while. Or we ask for one thing when we really want another. Regardless of the root causes, our channels of power become blocked when we cut off these two crucial things: the capacity to see others with a clear set of eyes and connection to our most genuine needs and desires.

Signs That Your Power Is Unplugged
- You are often disappointed or annoyed with others for not going along with your plan.
- People around you comply but their energy is flat.
- You struggle with ambivalence or indecision.
- When you make requests of others you are already annoyed or angry.
- You share a lot about the things that you don't like or don't want.
- You offer others the opportunity to make most decisions.
- People ask you for advice but then they argue with you or don't listen.
- You often feel ignored, sidelined, or not consulted.
- You feel sorry for yourself.
- You carry around a fair amount of resentment toward others.
- On the rare occasion you do ask for things and others provide, you feel guilty.
- You often sign up to do things out of obligation or duty.

Signs Your Control Muscle Is Overdeveloped
- You feel like no one understands you.
- People are always telling you what to do.
- You often feel lonely and unsupported.
- You aren't sure that you can trust others.

- Other people used to be there for you, but they have disappeared.
- You feel sorry for yourself.
- People don't have good boundaries with you, and you feel like a doormat.
- You don't like letting people do nice things for you.
- It's hard to accept compliments.

Think of your control muscle as a gate. If we are overcontrolled, we mostly keep our gate closed or even locked. We don't allow anyone in. If we are undercontrolled, our gate is wide open, and others walk all over us. Most of us need to recalibrate our control system so that we can make more intentional choices about what influences we allow in and when to have better boundaries about influences that have no business in our lives.

Power and Control Imbalances Create Drama

Conflict is inherent in all mammal relationships. Any time there are multiple individuals with varying needs and limited resources, a negotiation will need to occur. Conflict is not necessarily a negative thing; however, when power and control are out of balance in our relationships, conflict escalates. We need a healthy balance of power and control in order to resolve conflict. With other mammals, when conflict isn't able to resolve, situations can become physically dangerous, either with violence or with the fracturing of an intact group, which can lead to life-threatening isolation or loss of access to necessary resources. Humans play this out a bit differently. Though our unresolved conflicts can lead to physical altercations, more often than not, we become much more entrenched in the emotional and relational story, or what we refer to as drama.

Drama is a state, situation, or series of events involving interesting or intense conflict or forces that catch our attention and pull us in. We are attracted to drama because, let's face it, it can be entertaining. We can experience big emotional states, which we crave when we are bored or depressed. We can also engage in drama to create a neurological state change when we are in pain. Drama, whether we are witnessing or participating in conflict, will recruit adrenaline and other numbing chemicals involved in our survival functioning. We can crave drama the same way we long for other escape behaviors or substances. Engaging or indulging in interpersonal conflict can fulfill an unmet need for community and kinship. Even when it's unhealthy behavior like gossip or arguing, we will seek connection rather than feel isolated or alone.

The Food Chain Impact

Once human animals stopped hunting and gathering for survival, we no longer inhabited an entirely wild ecosystem. We began domesticating plants and animals and altering landscapes to support domesticated species. In the process, we began to become domesticated ourselves, as animals, with much less connection to our inner wildness. Our human ego likes to put us at the top of the food chain. In many ways, because of our weaponry, protection, and advanced brains, we are now superpredators. But we have a wild animal within us that is both hunter and hunted. Predation is hardwired into our mammal bodies and in our genetic coding. Our awareness as a prey animal is baked into our primitive being. When the predator and prey positions become salient, a one-up and one-down bifurcation occurs, and a power struggle ensues. While some of the inherent predator/prey patterns we possess can help us in contemporary human life, they can also get us into big trouble.

Here are some examples:

- Us vs. them mindset
- Intimidation or bullying behaviors
- Obsessing and overanalyzing details
- Using fear as a tactic to get our way
- Overworking or pushing too hard toward accomplishments
- Seeing the world as out to get us
- Revenge behaviors and holding grudges
- Difficulty building trusting relationships

The Cost of Drama

Drama mindsets and behaviors drain our time, focus, and energy, making us less able to perform and achieve in our personal and professional lives. Because drama perpetuates conflict and blocks solutions, it causes stress and tension, which have physical and psychological consequences. Ongoing drama will begin to define relationships, and the negative patterns will begin to dominate, causing irreparable damage to the trust and safety in our relationships. In the end, drama prevents people from learning to work and live well with others and gets in the way of developing core relational competencies and problem-solving skills.

The Drama Triangle

In the late 1960s, psychiatrist Stephen Karpman conceived of The Drama Triangle, a social model or template that helps us understand conflict in our human relationships. He observed that when people are in conflict, or are hurt and/or scared, we drop into "good guy vs. bad guy" thinking. He also observed that people become drawn in, even seduced, by the energy that the drama generates. The drama obscures the real issues. Confusion and emotional upset escalate. People are no longer able to focus on solutions. Karpman defined three roles in The Drama Triangle: Persecutor/Villain (one-up position), Rescuer/Hero (one-up position), and Victim (one-down position). Karpman placed these three roles on an inverted triangle and described them as being the three aspects, or faces, of drama. When people are in the one-up positions of Villain or Hero, they are overpowering the Victim, even if they are trying to be helpful. Typically, when people are in the one-down position of Victim, they are overcontrolled and blocking any influence, movement, or help. This is why a victim mindset can sound so helpless and hopeless at times.

THE DRAMA TRIANGLE

adapted from Stephen Karpman

VILLAIN
This is your fault.
You shouldn't have done it like that.
There's only one right way to to this.
I'm in charge. I know best.
I better take over.
You don't know what you're doing.
She/he is incompetent.
They caused this whole mess.

HERO
I can help.
I'm always here to listen or give advice.
I'm the best one to solve this problem.
I know how to do that.
No one else is willing to help so I will.
I can save you.
I am willing to try anything to fix this.
She/he needs me.
I'm the only one who understands.

VICTIM
It's not fair. I didn't have a choice.
I have such a hard time making decisions.
I feel so helpless.
It's all hopeless.
I don't know what to do.
Bad things keep happening to me.
I get so overwhelmed.
No one understands me and how hard this is.

As long as there are people, there will be drama. There is no way to stop drama from happening or to prevent yourself from being pulled into it from time to time. Rooted to the natural elements of power and control, The Drama Triangle is the human creation of our mammalian survival roots, the characters and story of the food chain. However, there are tools we can use to help ourselves notice when we're getting pulled into drama or when we're creating it and trying to pull others into drama. We can look at where our power and control have become imbalanced, and we can identify The Drama Triangle position we might be playing so we can opt into a new mindset and new relational behaviors. For decades, people have created successful models for a drama alternative. Many of them play on the topic of empowerment. The following is a version of an Empowerment Triangle, which flips The Drama Triangle so that the only way to inhibit the one-up position is with openness and vulnerability.

EMPOWERMENT TRIANGLE

I AM AN OPEN BOOK
I let you know who I am, what I need/want, how I struggle. I ask for support and help. I am open about my experience in our relationship. I'm willing to risk being vulnerable because I want you to know the real me.

OPENNESS & TRANSPARENCY

I TRUST MYSELF AND I TAKE CARE OF MYSELF
I hold myself accountable for my own emotions, thoughts, and actions. I commit to express myself when needed.

CURIOSITY & COMPASSION

RESPONSIBILITY & ASSERTIVENESS

I SEEK TO UNDERSTAND
I listen and learn without judgement. I put my own story aside so I can understand yours.

How to Check Your Power and Control Balance

Think about an aspect of your personal or professional life that matters a great deal to you: a project, goal, or a relationship. You are going to use this as your topic to explore your power and control balance. Like all aspects of our self-leadership, more awareness of our tendencies helps us to be better prepared for how we might misstep in our relationships.

Start by making two lists:

1. This first list will consist of the areas in which you doubt you have influence. Think of the issues, actions, processes, and behaviors you cannot move forward, progress, or change.
2. This second list will consist of the areas where you believe **you are able to effect change,** influence, and impact.

All of us have some degree of power and control imbalance. It's very helpful to figure out the way it's most likely to play out so we can become more aware and prepared for it. As you go through your lists, label each item with one of these imbalance themes:

- **Overpowered:** I muscle or bulldoze others in order to move things forward.
- **Underpowered:** I believe and/or act as if I don't have any influence to move things forward.
- **Overcontrolled:** I am actively protecting or guarding myself from being bulldozed by others.
- **Undercontrolled:** I feel bulldozed or flooded by others and there's nothing I can do about it.

Now, see if you can identify your dominant theme. How are you most likely to be out of balance? Go back to your topic and spend a bit of time challenging your story, patterns, and beliefs. You will have to push through some resistance here. When it comes to power and control, we can become a bit fossilized in our thinking and our behavior.

Try to generate three to five ways you could create more balance. If you are typically overpowered, how could you let up and reduce the pressure a bit? If you are underpowered, how might you push yourself and/or ask more of others? If you are overcontrolled, look for ways you can open the gate and allow things to move or others to influence you. If you are undercontrolled, where are you needing some boundaries and preferences of your own?

The Practice: Moving into Empowerment

1. Read this script all the way through and notice the positions on The Drama Triangle noted in parentheses. As you read through, circle the statements that you would be most likely to say out loud to another person.

   Sue: I can't believe you forgot to make dinner! (P)
   Bill: Well, I had a ton of work to finish. My team needed me to get things done by the end of day. (R)
   Sue: You work too much! (P)
   Bill: You wouldn't want me to lose my job, would you? My whole career could crash, and we could lose everything. (V)
   Sue: Your team can certainly function without you. (P)
   Bill: I just didn't want them to feel like I abandoned them. (R)
   Sue: You know, that's the problem with having a young team. They expect you, as the leader, to do everything. (P)
   Bill: That's only natural. They are just young and learning. (R)
   Sue: I work like a dog all day at a job I hate. (V)

Bill: Yes, I know. You are such a hard worker. I'm sorry. (R)

Sue: And now I don't even have anything to eat! (V)

Bill: I can cook something now! It won't take too long. (R)

Sue: Have you even looked at the clock? It's almost bedtime. (P)

Bill: Well maybe if you shared some of our household responsibilities, we'd have something to eat! (P)

Sue: You never told me you felt burdened. How am I supposed to know? (P)

Bill: As if you don't see me doing everything. You never notice my efforts. (P)

Sue: I'm just exhausted. You don't know what it's like to be a working mom. (V)

Bill: Right. I don't know what it's like to be a working parent. (P)

2. Now you know your dominant position on The Drama Triangle, or the position in which you are most likely to enter into drama. This awareness can help you to more quickly recognize when you have gotten pulled into drama.

3. Pick one relationship in your personal or professional life in which you:
   - Feel stressed and/or frustrated
   - Find yourself in conflict
   - Feel manipulated
   - Wonder if you can trust the other person
   - Question your own integrity or motives
   - Think of a recent interaction in which you played that role. Now use The Empowerment Triangle and write

at least three statements that could have gotten you out of drama.

4. You're going to hate this part. Read those statements out loud. That's right! It really helps to rehearse a new role so we can get through the awkwardness and unfamiliarity of a new script.

5. You've found the place where you need the most practice and strength-building. Look for places to use the empowered position as much as you can. Notice how you feel about yourself when you shift out of drama and into empowerment.

6. Think of a person you are leading (at work, children, students, clients, etc.). Are you in drama in those relationships? How could you pivot into empowerment when you are in your leadership role or helper role?

CHAPTER EIGHT

Desire

All human activity is prompted by desire. Civilized life has grown altogether too tame, and, if it is to be stable, it must provide harmless outlets for the impulses which our remote ancestors satisfied in hunting. Pains should be taken to provide constructive outlets for the love of excitement. Nothing in the world is more exciting than a moment of sudden discovery or invention, and many more people are capable of experiencing such moments than is sometimes thought.

BERTRAND RUSSELL

Creativity is an attempt to resolve a conflict generated by unexpressed biological impulses, such that unfulfilled desires are the driving force of the imagination, and they fuel our dreams and daydreams.

SIGMUND FREUD

The Story: More Play and Less Nay

We're standing on the expansive hills of Zamora, California, and I have an earpiece dangling on the side of my head, stuck in my hair. I can't seem to get the pesky thing to stay in my ear, although I'm still able to hear Bill's voice in spite of that. There's too much dog and sheep action to stop and fix it, so I carry on as best as I can. I'm here with my yearling Border Collie, Georgie, and we're taking her sheep work to the next level. It's a far bigger space for us, with more hills, and a sizably larger flock than we've ever worked. Fortunately, I have help, the trusted guidance of an accomplished and well-respected sheepdog trainer. I haven't worked with him for a while, and this is his first time seeing my young dog. The landscape is a quirky combination of Scottish hills and the barren surfaces of Mars you see in NASA images—endless expanses with no trees in sight. When the north wind picks up in these hills, the gusts can be relentless.

I was forewarned that Georgie might reveal a different side of herself in this new and exciting environment. It's only the second time she's been off our ranch to work sheep, and young dogs are likely to blow a gasket with the novelty and stimulation of it all. So far, it's going well, even better than at home. Bill's been offering direction and helping us set things up so we can see where she is in her learning. He's told me a couple of times not to correct her. I hear his words yet find myself puzzled. I call Georgie's name when she seems to have given up her focus and has become consumed, almost enamored, by the speed of her own body. I shout *"Hey!"* when she's rushing the sheep. *Is that a correction? Am I a corrector?* I ponder judgmentally. Bill keeps telling me to give her direction. He says she's further along than I realize, and he comments about how nice she is, how capable, how willing. Georgie is a daughter to one of his beloved dogs, and I can hear his joy in watching her work. I find myself gloating in the praise as if it's about me. I can feel my ego invested. And then he stops us and says we should take a break and talk.

I walk along the steep ravine toward Bill and happily struggle to adjust the earpiece in my tangled hair. As I approach, he says, "You don't have to correct a dog like Georgie. In fact, you don't want to correct a dog like her much at all." I think, *How am I going to train her if I can't correct her? What else am I supposed to do?* Then he adds, "When you correct a dog, you leave it up to them to figure out what you actually want. All you're doing is telling them what you don't want. It's a dead end. There's so much value in giving her commands." And there is the triggering word: *commands.* I hear it and know immediately what I'm up against. This is my issue. It's everywhere.

"I haven't wanted to give commands because I don't want to overpressure the relationship before she's ready."

Bill smirks a bit and says, "Pressure is inherent. It's just a matter of what kind of pressure you want to introduce and what kind of partnership you want." Right. *What kind of partnership do I want?*

I've spent a decade trying to uncover and recover some semblance of female leadership in its purest mammal form, not the bastardized and misguided female imitation of male leadership. It's been hard to find role models in the human world. So, I've taken to studying horses, to watching my mares as they commit and maintain a stable matriarchy. It's been so pleasurable that I've collected more mares over the years and even refer to my herd as Mareadise, as their culture has a safety like nothing I've ever known. I spend hours grazing alongside them to take in and become part of the energy they transmit. It's serene, but it's also fiercely powerful, sensitive, and responsive. They have a feedback system that so clearly communicates each other's desires and needs. They are wholly honest and direct.

As my first female Border Collie, Georgie has been helping me see the female leadership commonalities in the dog pack and the similar roles we play as females in the world of mammals. Georgie is a dynamo. I could see it early on, feel it in her intense eye and the precision with which she moves through the world. When she stops, she lays her body down so fast and hard that she sometimes rolls herself like a ball player sliding into home base a millisecond before the ball reaches the catcher's mitt. She's the kind of dog who wants to please. She thrives with a job well done, pauses to revel for just a moment, and then asks for another task. She is an eager and attentive listener, and she loves to learn. But she wants the lesson once, and only once. I suppose you could categorize her as a perfectionist or an overachiever, personality traits I know all too well. She's a Border Collie and these characteristics aren't unusual for the breed, but some dogs are turbocharged and super-powered. Georgie is one of those dogs.

I have admired the exquisite mix of fortitude and sensitivity in Georgie, and I've been committed all along to respecting her leadership, giving adequate space for her to find herself. But in this moment standing on a hillside, I'm struggling to cross the threshold into my own fully embodied and committed leadership. I need to give commands. I need to set direction. I need to tell my dog what I want. *Why is this so hard? Why do I hold back?* I know what I want. My vision is clear. But I judge it as bossy and controlling. I'm too much. I'll create a shadow that others will get lost in. I put 10 percent out into the world and stuff the rest. Things unfold. And then I correct or quietly sit in disappointment. Wash. Rinse. Repeat.

"You do that enough times and a dog like Georgie will start to tighten up and get twitchy," Bill says. I'm listening. And I know. I can immediately track the dozens of scenarios and relationships that I've impacted with correction instead of command. He must see the stress on my face as I dread that I've damaged my connection with Georgie. "Beth, you guys are just getting started. Switch gears. It's simple. Tell her what you want." I can see it. I can visualize the path forward and it's like a rush of possibility and freedom pulsing through my veins. My own body has more energy. My mind is racing. I've had no idea how bottlenecked I've been. The connections are lighting up, and I can see all of the places in my life where I'm holding back in fear of micromanaging others or impeding their freedom. I remember a sticky note I used to have posted above my desk. An incredibly helpful therapist worked with me for a couple of years on the difference between disappointment and desire. The note read: *That which I see that I don't like. Or what I am wanting in this moment.*

I've been watching Georgie wade around in the water trough drinking and cooling herself. The late afternoon clouds mute the sun's vibrancy. I zip up my vest and put my hands in my pockets, as if to gather up my body and my spirit for what comes next. I call her to me, and we head through the gate for another go. This time I know what is needed—for Georgie, for myself, for our partnership. With a focused awareness, I can see exactly what I want. The commands roll off my tongue like the words of a favorite song, second nature and full of joy. Georgie is on fire; her body moves with more ease than ever before. She listens like her life depends on it and we're entirely connected. The more I open to my desire, the better I can read her. Our feedback loop gains its own momentum and becomes a dance. I begin to feel the playfulness in it. More play and less nay. In these gentle hills, I begin to explore more of me, to own and claim a missing element of my own maturity, like a rock that I've been clumsily kicking down the road.

When is it in our lives, in our stories, that it becomes unsafe or painful to want? When do we begin to curb our desire? We take our dogs to the big hills because it opens them up, widens their perspective. The geography and natural contours teach them scope better than any human lesson can. You can literally watch their bodies change, extend, and expand as they navigate the terrain and feel their own power. I take myself to these same hills to learn alongside my dog and to begin to trust the power of my desire, to feel the freedom of it. I imagine that when you watch us, you see the change in me too.

The Concept: Shifting from Disappointment to Desire

Emotions serve a life-giving, lifesaving, and life-fulfilling purpose for all mammals, including humans. Our emotional system acts as a bridge between us and the world around us, and it is the drumbeat and bassline of our relational world. Our emotions alert us to what we need and to what others need. They also let us know what we want and don't want. Just like our physical sensations keep us safe and alert, our emotions signal us; however, we have gotten into a long-standing habit, as humans, of judging and not listening to or trusting our emotions. Decades of social conditioning have molded us and told us that succumbing to our feelings makes us weak. So, we go to great lengths to suppress our emotions.

Disappointment, which is a human construct, is an emotional and cognitive thinking pattern. It is one of the ways we bypass making use of raw feelings and the important energy they provide to us. While disappointment does have some emotional ingredients, such as fear, anger, or sadness, it is more rooted in thoughts of judgment and scorn. It serves as a protective layer from our more vulnerable emotions, and it does so by acting as an intellectual and other-focused veneer. It is blame-focused and tells a story about things outside of us that can help us to not feel the emotions that are going on inside of us. Our basic emotions signal to us about our needs and how to safely survive and thrive. For instance, panic tells us to run, and care tells us to nurture and love. One of the dangers of being led by disappointment is that it does not give us adequate or accurate signals about how to take action. If you look at the basic emotions of mammals, you'll see that disappointment is not one of them!

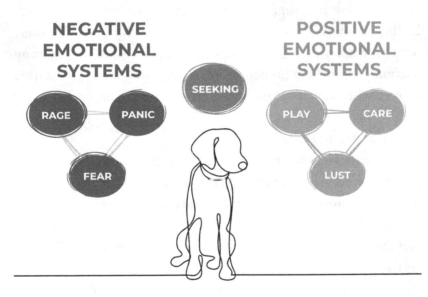

The Cost of Disappointment

If disappointment is a numbing agent of pain, it is also a numbing agent of desire, joy, and creativity. If you think about emotions as creating energy or blocking energy, disappointment is an energy blocker. It comes with a cost. You may feel less pain, but you will also feel less of everything else. Disappointment takes the wind out of our sails and creates apathy, malaise, depression, hopelessness, and fatigue.

We don't want to reject disappointment completely though. It's a common cognitive–emotional experience. So, when we notice that we are disappointed, it's best to do some discernment.

Here's the inquiry: *Is this disappointment telling me that I need to take care of myself or take some action with another person? Or is the disappointment going in circles and taking me with it?*

If disappointment is not serving an informative function about an action that is needed, then it is getting in the way of desire. It helps to think of disappointment as the signal before the signal. It's like a traffic light that turns yellow before it turns red. We don't want to ignore the signal. As disappointment is such a common phenomenon for the human mind, it's best to work with it rather than to wish it away or pretend it isn't impacting us.

Desire as a Life Force

Desire is an inherently creative force. It has its origins in our primitive impulse to squirm and crawl, or find a breast, or scream for care. It's the mammalian part of us that is resilient and survival-based. Freud referred to this in describing "drive." He noticed that the human mind could create "mental representations" of our nervous system activation. It sounds complicated, but in short, the animal body gets triggered by needs, which creates an energy that drives us to meet those needs.

As we become more sophisticated with our thinking and in our adult lives, that drive becomes our creative projects and our goals. But at the very core of it all is desire. Psychologist David Schnarch writes, "Wanting creates the space in which our highest aspirations come into being." This part of us, which has raw energy and immense power, is underutilized. We are painfully unskilled at accessing it. In fact, if we consider how we are educated and socialized, a lot of effort is made compartmentalizing desire, putting it in a box as if it ought to be hidden. This makes good sense in some ways. Our social norms rely on impulse control; however, as we know from a systemic approach to all natural elements, balance is key. We need to look at the ways that we may be curbing drives and impulses without making room for desire.

To begin to access our desire, we must move unhelpful or habitual disappointment out of the way. Without the disappointment there, we can ask this very powerful question: *What do I want in this moment?*

What Do I Want in This Moment?

It's raw, real, honest, life-giving, and at the heart of our leadership. You can probably tell, just from reading it, that the question lights us up inside. Accessing that question and voicing your answer to yourself and others creates energy within you and around you. It's visionary, forward-moving, and solution-focused. It empowers us and it gives others a chance to participate. It's a really important question.

The Vulnerability of Desire

We have so many human stories about the phenomenon of wanting. It is perhaps one of the most vulnerable human experiences to become aware of our own desires and then to share them with others. We risk and fear that we will be judged or rejected, or that we will suffer the disappointment of not having our desires met. "I want you to bring me a cup of coffee." Could that really have that much emotional weight? Well, you only have to look a few layers deep to see the meaning behind that ask and the many relational risks it encompasses. *I want you to take care of me. I want you to serve me. I want to lounge and luxuriate. I want to be lazy. I want you. I want. I want. I want.* There's no way to spin it. It's painful to be alone with unmet desire or to be judged for showing others who we are. Yet, the more we do it, the more resilient we get when our desire isn't met with open arms. Think of improvisational actors or musicians or creative teams and how many hundreds of times each person has to muster the guts to put forth ideas that may not be used. Resilience is the capacity to stay emotionally stable in the face of fear, failure, rejection, or pain. Like all our capacities, it can be expanded with use. Just like a muscle group. The more we put our desires out into the world, the better we get at being seen, regardless of the outcome.

Inviting Desire into the Animal Body

As soon as we begin to judge ourselves or modulate our desire, we cut off the flow of energy in our bodies. We see this all the time with people and horses when we do experiential workshops. Imagine this scenario: *You want the horse to come to you. You allow yourself that desire for a split second before you question yourself. Or maybe you are afraid that you are going to fail and not get what you want. The horse feels this, senses the point of confusion and pressure in your body, and won't come toward you. It is a brick wall of your own creation. As you work on letting go of those doubts or judgments, you can begin to reconnect with your desire. When the horse can feel a clear channel and invitation, he will walk right to you.* The desire a person feels in that moment is a point of reference and can become an internal template for future use. It's our Natural Leadership coming to life. We can thank our animal teachers for modeling it. When we don't have animals available, children also are great role models for us. They have access to the same open channel of desire, and they are very willing to give us honest feedback, both verbal and nonverbal, about the quality of our adult version of desire.

How to Lead with Inspired Energy

Let's get practical. The emotional and thought world of disappointment is like a dark alley with a dead end. It doesn't leave us many places to go, and when we are in that internal space, others can sense and feel it. When our animal body is communicating that kind of negative and immobilized energy, it is very hard to lead, relate, or influence. Many of us have disappointment habits, and we don't even realize how much of a role they're playing. The more we study ourselves and practice our self-leadership, the more aware and efficient we become unclearing blocked channels when they occur.

Consider the most charismatic and impactful people in your life. Think of teachers, coaches, bosses, or friends whose energy is infectious and who you want to be around. They let themselves be seen and known. And they invite you in. They are all in, and their commitment to authentic expression of themselves is palpable and attractive. They are "inspirational" because they have "spirit" flowing within them. Desire, in its purest form, is what drives that inspired energy. Psychoanalyst Jacques Lacan writes, "Desire, a function central to all human experience, is the desire for nothing nameable. And at the same time this desire lies at the origin of every variety of animation."

It's commonly recommended that when we lift something heavy, we pause and lift with our legs and core muscles. The same is true when we are self-aware leaders in our own lives or with others. Before any relational transaction, we can pause and determine if we are leading with the residue of disappointment or with the inspired energy of desire. Are we focused on the negative, the past, and things we don't like? Or are we in the present and moving forward with the natural volition of what we want?

The Practice: Finding the Object of Your Desire

Step One: The Disappointment Record

Similar to a thought record, a resentment and disappointment inventory will help you to discover more about yourself and to identify some habitual thinking, feeling, and relating patterns that you might not be aware of. Some of your automatic thoughts might fall into the category of resentment or disappointment and may not actually be serving you well. For one week, keep track in a notebook (paper or digital) of what your mind does in difficult situations or relationships in which you are struggling to get your needs met.

Identifying Resentments

If you think that someone has a pattern of hurting or wronging you, and you haven't cleared the air, it's likely that you have a resentment festering. Resentments are like unhealed wounds. Some hurts and wrongdoings require a relationship reset or a conversation in which openness and repair takes place. Other times, and for a variety of reasons, that isn't possible, so we need a process that allows us to let go of resentments so that they no longer negatively affect us.

Identifying Disappointments

Disappointments are similar to resentments in that they are situations in which someone has hurt or scared us. But disappointment differs in that it carries a layer of judgment and contempt. We take the hurt and add a hint of scorn or a low hum of anger. If someone has continued to hurt us over time, we become somewhat numb to the pain by adding judgment and anger. Disappointment keeps us a bit removed from the pain itself. Disappointments have less emotion than resentments. They are more like judgmental thoughts.

For the sake of the exercise, it doesn't matter if you differentiate between disappointments and resentments. Keep track of both! Whenever you notice a resentful or disappointed thought or feeling, write it down. You might notice some repetitive thoughts or feelings; write them down anyway. After you have a good week's worth of inventory, review the list to see if you can identify commonalities. Organize them into categories: themes, people, and situations.

As you go through the list, identify which thoughts and feelings are outdated, not useful, or simply habits. Now, go through the list and identify which of the thoughts and feelings call for your attention. Look for the resentments and disappointments that require action.

Working with Disappointment

1. When you notice you are going into one of your disappointment spaces, pause and do the disappointment inquiry: **Is this disappointment telling me that I need to take care of myself or take some action with another person? Or is the disappointment going in circles and taking me with it?**

2. If you find the disappointment is not useful and rooted in a past experience or automatic thought, gently tell yourself to let it go.

3. If you find the disappointment is calling for action, ask yourself the desire question: **What do I want in this moment?**

4. As you continue this process, make note of what happens in your body when you ask that question. Pay attention to the spark or flow or aliveness you feel. It's normal to feel a bit afraid or vulnerable.

The Desire Object

After you have done this process for a few days, you will feel more competent at it. You will get a feel for it and be able to more quickly and efficiently recognize your own internal patterns. Now, begin to look around your immediate world. See if you can find what we call The Object of Your Desire. This will be an object that becomes an important symbol for you. It will act as a reminder of your desire and how it helps you to move forward and ask for what you want and need.

An Example

My object of desire is a feather. Feathers have appeared at many interesting times in my life, and they have often been connected to situations that called for me to be fully alive as a leader of my life. My matriarchal energy is in the feather. The feather drops when no longer needed and is a great symbol of letting go. At the same time, the feather acts as a necessary part of flight and is essential for a bird to do its life tasks. Feathers are a great symbol of desire for me. Whether I desire letting go or taking flight, I look to the feather to help me drop into my Natural Leadership body.

CHAPTER NINE

Trust

The more we trust, the farther we are able to venture.
ESTHER PEREL

Courage is only an accumulation of small steps.
GEORGE KONRAD

This longing for a safe zone is one reason we pair up. However, partners—whether in a romantic relationship or committed friendship—often fail to use each other as advocates and allies against all hostile forces. They don't see the opportunities to make a home for one another; to create a safe place in which to relax and feel accepted, wanted, protected, and cared for.
STAN TATKIN

The Story: Sharing the Shade Tree

When I brought Sally to my ranch, she and Rosie experienced freedom and space together for the first time. They knew each other from the barn where they used to live and from horse shows where they both competed, but they hadn't spent much time together.

Life, for many horses, is run by human ideas. Our needs or our beliefs about what's best for the horse prescribe their lifestyle, so they spend much of their existence living in stalls with limited time to run, graze, roam free, or socialize with other horses. But horses are herd animals. In the wild, they spend all day, every day in constant companionship with their multigenerational families. They have an ancient system of relationships, or what we can call a culture. Although not all herds are the same, all herds do share the same commitment to trust as a fundamental need.

There are many equine myths I once believed that have been dispelled over time and through my experiences of living with my own herd. One misunderstanding about herd culture is that mares don't play. I thought it was true until I saw the high-spirited frolicking that emerged almost immediately after Sally and Rosie began to explore my fields together. It's true that mares don't play like stallions or geldings. And they don't play like youngsters. But most mares love to run together, throwing their necks and manes into the wind and into each other, their heels into the air as they float above the ground in sweeping circles. Their play is boisterous, big, and committed. They bring their whole selves to the party, and they lean into the collective nature of the activity. Play is done together, an opportunity to feed off each other's energy, to co-create, and to sync individual bodies into one unit of motion and speed.

The moment when I first witnessed the passionate play between Rosie and Sally moved me to tears. It brought me back to when I was a young girl in love with all things horse. I didn't always want to own a horse. Sometimes I wanted to *be* a horse. Those were the options: either be with the horse or be the horse. I would gallop through the tall grass in the back meadow of my childhood home in Michigan, tossing my chestnut mane and snorting into the sky. As I watched Rosie and Sally, I wanted to be out there with them, longing to run and frolic. Frolic is the best word to describe mare play. It has an irresistible energy, a pull to join in and to do whatever it takes to make your human form more equine.

Rosie and Sally developed a daily routine, a circuit of sorts that spanned the pasture space. Their activities were determined by needs: water, food, shade, movement, and rest. The horse body and digestive system has a natural rhythm that is designed to graze approximately twenty out of twenty-four hours per day. Movement and free foraging are essential to their basic needs. So, they sleep in twenty-minute increments, only four hours per day. Prey animal life requires more vigilance in order to stay safe in a world of predators. It seemed, from my vantage point, that the mares took turns leading each other through their daily meanderings, suggesting naps or rests as they moved in and out of shade and sun. I looked out of my windows often to catch glimpses of them standing, head to tail, sharing the responsibility of fly control. Sometimes I'd see their heads together, dipped as if in prayer, muzzles almost touching, two mares in the shape of a heart.

After about six months of companionship, the Rosie-and-Sally friendship had burgeoned and become unshakeable. The trust and ease they had built was breathtaking. In my relationship with Rosie, I found a depth in our connection that reached a new place of trust and love within me. Once Sally became part of our world, I realized that loyalty and relationships between mares were bottomless and soulful. Female friendships in the human world can be quite complicated, perhaps made so by multiple generations lacking positive examples. Ridden with competition and infighting, it's as if girls and women have lost their natural instincts to circle up and lean on each other. I had known my own mistrust and heartache in adolescent friendships that were cruel and often frightening. But the fabric of this mare friendship began to show me something new. Trust was the very first thing these mares attended to. They fashioned their bond and then guarded it as if their lives depended on it.

Around that time, my daughter Emma started riding lessons from a wonderful instructor who had a large pony. It turned out his name was Levi. It made perfect sense to me that Emma's first love affair with a horse would be the namesake of my first Border Collie. After a sweet afternoon of riding and grooming, Emma finished decorating Levi's long mane with dozens of bows and barrettes. She wrapped her arms around his narrow chest and told him that he was her best friend. You could see, in his eyes and slowness of his breath, that he answered her back. He, too, was in love. When her riding teacher asked if we wanted to take Levi home for a visit, it was pretty obvious that I had no choice!

We unloaded Levi from the horse trailer, and he stood proud and alert, tail flagged in the air, his pinto body throwing flashes of color in every direction. Half Arabian and half something else, Levi would often prance and snort and toss his luxurious mane across his shoulders. We joked that Levi acted like an Arabian horse for about five minutes and then he became a sleepy, kid-friendly pony who specialized in little girls. He was about the most dependable barn babysitter you could ask for. He knew how to make himself smaller almost like he folded his body in half in order to meet Emma and her preschool friends at their level. It didn't take long for me to trust him, wholly, deeply, and with as much gratitude as I had for our dear dog, Glen, who shared Emma's crib with her every morning.

When Sally and Rosie came to greet the horse trailer and our new guest, they were excited. It's an incredibly exciting event when new horses visit. They were curious and friendly, but they were also unsure. You could see the mares working together to size him up, so much body language and posturing as they moved about and walked the fence line to get closer. They didn't chase him off or lunge at the fence, which can sometimes happen. But the feedback dance began immediately as they assessed his demeanor. They began to teach him the rules of the ranch according to mares—their rules. This is Mareadise, after all. And Sally and Rosie are the stewards.

Levi acted like a gentleman. After his five minutes of flaunting his fanciness, he quieted and returned to his usual soft eye with no drama or posturing. In fact, his attitude seemed respectful as if to say, "Yes, ma'am. I do understand that this place is yours. How may I be of service to you?" They shared a fence line for a few days, a good practice that creates a physical boundary to allow the horses to settle in and get to know each other without the pressure of interacting. When it seemed likely that everyone would get along, I opened the gates and let the horses become a little herd. The mares were welcoming and invited him to join them. Rosie initiated a frolic, which Levi loved with immense enthusiasm. For about five minutes.

In the mid-afternoon, Rosie and Sally made their way to their favorite shade tree, a black walnut in the middle of the corral closest to the barn. This particular spot was a great place to rest in the most intense heat of the afternoon, with adequate sun cover and the northern wind that blew right through the branches at the exact time the mares settled into their napping positions. Rosie and Sally had a definite routine and an exact configuration. They were fully committed to it, and they invited Levi to learn it alongside them.

But when Levi tried to join them at the shade tree, he got some immediate and direct feedback. Ears back and tails swishing, both mares told him to back off. He slowed down a bit. But it wasn't quite responsive enough, so Rosie chased him off and took a small but meaningful bite on his rump as he puttered off. Sally pinned her ears and gave him a sour look, just to make a point. He slowed to a stop and hung his head, taking cues from the mares about nap time. We all learned quickly that Levi was always up for a nap. The mares settled into their usual positions in the shade and Levi stood in the sun, close by but with the space Rosie had created with her very clear boundaries.

I wanted to ensure this trio was progressing into a cohesive herd and that all was staying safe, so I checked in throughout the day from various windows, just watching as they made their way through the pastures and followed their daily routine. At the same time each day, the conversation at the shade tree occurred. I began to look forward to it, to study it. Each day, Levi would ask the mares, mostly Rosie, if he could step another twelve to fifteen inches toward the shade. If he went slow and waited, the mares would allow it. If he went too fast or covered too much ground, they would block him in order to stop him or they would send him back a few feet. If he didn't listen attentively and wasn't responsive enough, he would have a much bigger setback. Then, the next day he'd start again. Slow and steady was the name of the game. But sometimes he would get carried away and forget the rules. The mares never forgot the rules.

It wasn't that the mares didn't want him or didn't like him. It wasn't that there wasn't enough room to share the shade. In fact, as I learned later, Levi's presence as a protector was of huge value to the mares. Something different was happening at this tree. At that time of the day, the tree was the most valued resource, and the mares' configuration was built on trust and shared space, and it was something they cherished and guarded. That moment in time and space provided the most powerful opportunity for each animal to clearly express their needs, their preferences, and to pay attention to those expressions so they could learn about each other. They wanted to share the space, but they needed to stitch together micromoments of shared needs in order to build trust. It wasn't about the shade. It was about the conversation, about developing a fluency in their relational language.

With every expression of needs and request for space or closeness, each animal had the chance to relax into more ease. Levi was asking to join the herd. Sally and Rosie were saying, "Maybe. Let's see. Let's see how this goes and how you adapt to the culture we've created." Sure, they wanted shade and a comfortable arrangement for napping. But it was more about creating a feedback system. The shade tree was the perfect environment for that to develop. The rules of the herd were about listening and respecting needs. No drama. No conflict. Sally and Rosie had created the culture, and it was built on trust.

It took a full four weeks for Levi to make it into the shade. But once he did, he stayed. That conversation was over. The spatial arrangement was resolved. And, most importantly, they had learned how to operate in their relationships. The culture was set. Two new herd members were later integrated in very much the same way, and Levi's role became clearer. At times he was sentry, protector. Sally and Rosie would send him to guard the perimeter and to hold the sacred space of the herd, to stay alert enough to guard. The herd learned that he was also a fantastic groomer and always eager to give a back scratch or a neck massage. He was also quite skilled in the art of rest and relaxation. He was the first to suggest a nap and to wait for Sally's acceptance. His relaxed and laid-back temperament was calming and helped the mares, especially Rosie, to settle when her vigilant temperament had her overly busy or unnecessarily upset. Levi was like a deep sigh or the perfect breeze.

When Sally had a foal, the culture of the herd had to shift. Needs changed dramatically. Overnight, Sally's needs were different, urgent, and driven by a primal energy that she was only beginning to feel and navigate as a first-time mother. There was a nursing colt, Moonshine, who had to discover the world, and his needs were entirely new to the group. I was reminded that many domesticated horses live in barn situations that don't allow for natural herd life. It's not uncommon for our typical horses, as pets, to be unfamiliar with the movements and rhythms of the equine life cycle because it has been so dramatically interfered with by humans. Some horses have only known their own youth, not the early days, weeks, and months of other young horses coming into the world. I watched the herd greet Sally's colt with wild exuberance and even a bit of confusion. In an effort to respect Sally's needs, I gave her and her colt some space and allowed each herd member to individually acquaint themselves with Moonshine.

I had been working with a client at the back of the ranch doing a leadership session during which the client has the unique opportunity to interact with the horses and to learn the nonverbal language of Natural Leadership. The client had chosen Levi and spent the better part of an hour struggling to get him to move when she asked him to, or to respect her personal space when she expressed a boundary. He was not, by any means, unsafe, but he was his usually languid self, slumbering about and taking little naps. She became more and more frustrated as this went on, the heat of the midday sun baking on our backs. I asked her, "Is this what is showing up at work? Does your team listen when you ask for something important?"

She stood there, the wound of her ineffectiveness written all over her face, and her mouth dropped open. "This is exactly what has been happening. They listen, nod, and then just don't move. Nothing moves forward. Even if I tell them it's a priority." We spent another thirty minutes working through more of this narrative and found some of the places within her that were blocked, some of the story and the emotional channels that were getting in the way of how she was communicating and leading. She had been holding back in her leadership. It had created quite a log jam.

I noticed Sally and Moonshine had been standing nearby, almost like they were watching the client as she progressed through her experience. We finished up and walked with Levi toward the barn. Levi was the only herd member who hadn't spent time with Sally and her new colt. Since I had him right there, I figured I'd put him in their corral and give them some time together. As I closed the gate, Moonshine perked up and trotted toward Levi. Their ears and eyes met with equal enthusiasm. You could really feel how excited they were to be sharing physical space. Sally gave Levi a series of quick feedback signals, one right after the other, as if to say, "Slow down. Stop. Back off. No. Hey. I said no." Levi, in his usual happy-go-lucky manner, had a dull to nonexistent response. It was like he didn't even notice her communication. And in one swift moment, she backed into him, and double barrel kicked him in the chest a dozen times. He leapt into action and made it to the other side of the corral in half a second.

"Oh my!" my client yelped.

"Yikes!" I said, as my eyes scanned over Levi's body.

Grateful Sally wasn't wearing horseshoes, I saw Levi only had a few superficial scrapes to his hind, but no blood was drawn. "He's okay. He'll be a bit sore perhaps but he's good," I told my client. Levi's eyes were wide and his body language much more alert than he had been before. He stood a moment and then licked and chewed, indicating that his nervous system had switched back into a rest and digest state. The threat was over. He lowered his head and looked to Sally. She licked and chewed and lowered her head. Moonshine nursed at her side, seeking sustenance but also the comfort of his mom's closeness after a moment of upset. Levi began a very deliberate and watchful journey toward Sally. She continued with her feedback, slowing him down a few times, but allowing him to approach. Before long, Levi and Moonshine were touching noses, as Sally observed. Levi nuzzled Moonshine and allowed him to tuck into his neck. Sally approved.

My client and I stood at the gate and watched. It was a beautiful display of leadership in action, of a feedback system built on honesty, directness, and a commitment to responsiveness.

"So, this is what it looks like when you give clear feedback and follow through," my client said, her face in awe.

"Yes, that's exactly what happened here. Sally needed Levi to listen. It's essential to her needs. It always has been. It's just that her needs have changed now that she has a baby. She was trying to tell him to pay attention and learn the new routine. And he was too slow to respond so there was a breach in their trust," I explained.

The trio navigated the corral together. Levi was a student of Sally's and Moonshine's needs, taking notes as he figured out his new role. He had gotten comfortable in their trust relationship, as he should have. But he needed to sharpen up in order to adapt with the changing herd. From that day forward, Levi became fully committed as Moonshine's babysitter and mentor. Sally oversaw the relationship and gave direction, but it was Levi who was most attentive to the colt. Sally and Levi never had another altercation. It doesn't serve a mammal group to linger in conflict. They renegotiated their relationship and added some new rules to the culture. Once those were understood and learned, they could move on. The phenomenon of moving on is a fundamental need in mammal life and in the natural world.

We watched as Sally moved on, letting go of any tension or upset toward Levi. We watched as Levi moved on and his body loosened and softened after the physical boundaries of Sally's kicks. We watched as Moonshine moved on and fell in love with another member of his herd, his family. We watched and we moved on, both me and my client holding an important lesson about how trust is at the heart of everything.

The Concept: Feedback and Shaping Relationships

Humans have an innate mammal signal system that helps us pick up on changes in our environment and on subtle cues from other humans, and to attend to nonverbal feedback. Our human-to-human communication is comprised of 55 percent body language, 38 percent tone of voice, and 7 percent language. This means that our overemphasis on language leaves us at a dramatic disadvantage if we want to be conscious, compassionate, and relationally agile.

A simple and usable definition of feedback is as follows: a system (verbal and nonverbal) that humans use to teach each other about how they want to be treated and how they want their cultures to operate. All other mammals use constant feedback in their groups to express needs, share resources, establish boundaries, and minimize energy spent on conflict. Efficiency in nature is a survival trait. Distractions from unnecessary upset or role confusion can create life-or-death situations. For humans, more frequent honest feedback can reduce stress, anxiety, isolation, loss of efficiency, operational chaos, and erosion of relationships.

Feedback as a Practice

Just like an athlete prepares for a game or a musician has a routine before performance, we can prepare to be a stable and responsible deliverer or receiver of feedback. We each have different ways to get ourselves grounded, calm, and clearheaded. It's important to do that pre-feedback work if you want to prevent your own upset and be prepared for the possibility of it with others.

New relationships need an intentional conversation about how to give and receive feedback in a way that can build trust. We call this Relational Onboarding. Taking the time for Relational Onboarding sets the groundwork for future communication, brings values of trust and psychological safety into focus, and helps people get to know each other more deeply. We can streamline the way we give each other feedback and create communication shortcuts when we spend time talking through a strategy and accounting for each other's sensitivities.

At any time, we can shift patterns and alter our feedback system in an already existing relationship. We might discover we have developed a way of relating with colleagues, friends, students, or family members that we need or want to change. This requires some conversation and may need to include repairing areas in the relationship where there has been disappointment or resentment.

The cadence and frequency of feedback is also important to attend to. We need ongoing microfeedback to let others know what is working well, what we need to shift, and places in which there are pressure or pain points to relieve. On any given day, our needs change, and frequent communication creates context for others to understand how to interact with us.

Feedback and Emotional Reactivity

Giving and receiving feedback can cause emotional upset for a few important reasons: bruised egos, fear of losing something we have, fear of not getting something we think we need, misunderstanding, and unexpected or shocking information. We can work on managing our own emotional storms when giving and receiving feedback and, by doing so, help whoever we are interacting with to feel safer and/or calmer. Emotional upset is contagious. The human brain picks up on heightened emotions and mirrors what those around us are feeling. Knowing this and staying aware allows us to hold onto our emotional leadership and sometimes steer another person or a group out of rough waters. Remember, our mammal nervous system is designed to sync up with the calmest and most stable nervous system nearby. It's in the best interest of our survival and our relational health to regulate our emotions quickly and efficiently.

When we slow down and listen deeply, we can maintain a curious mindset, which gives us a chance to ask questions and understand situations more deeply. Often, when people are in a feedback process, they are in a fear state and want desperately to get out of it. But if we commit to inquiry, we can gain more clarity about the feedback being offered. A curious mind recruits our higher brain structures, which we need in order to solve problems, consider cause and effect, plan for change, and self-reflect. Asking questions can help us stay out of our more primitive and reactive brain areas.

Feedback During Change

During times of conflict or confusion, our feedback systems are put to the test. Groups that make a commitment to trust-building behaviors when things are tense are more likely to move through those situations quickly and with minimal damage to relationships. This calls for self-reflection, everyone making an honest assessment of our part in problems, open and vulnerable sharing with others about our own mistakes or relational missteps and focus on getting to the other side of issues with a sense of cohesion and community. It also requires that we share openly if others have upset us, when a new piece of feedback is needed, and if there is something new, we would like to create in the relationship. There is a fine line between productive feedback and a blaming and shaming approach. We know when we are in a healthy feedback system if we are owning our part of the issue at hand and offering feedback with a sense of hope and creativity coming from within. If frustration or judgment underlies our feedback, we will deliver information to others that comes with baggage and causes harm to relationships.

What Are Boundaries and Why Do We Need Them?

While feedback is the system that creates the fabric of trust in relationships, boundaries are the interpersonal microcommunications that we use to shape relationships and to express our needs and preferences so that others can learn who we are and how to relate with us. We use boundaries in our relationships so that we can teach others how we want to be treated. This is how we set norms in a relationship. We're often delayed in knowing it's time to communicate our needs to others, however. So, aggravation or anger will alert us. But long before those spicy emotions emerge, we experience pressure. This is one of the many reasons that pressure, as a fundamental signal system, is so important and helpful for us to fine-tune.

Boundaries are fundamental to how we share space and resources. Without them, our relationships and groups are often in a state of confusion or even fear. When clear boundaries are part of our usual functioning, anxieties and tensions are much lower. Imagine an untrained puppy having a whole house to run around while her people are away for the day. Without structure, companionship, guidance, or cues about how to move through the day, she would feel insecure and not know how to take care of herself. Now, imagine six untrained puppies and no adult dog. Without boundaries and mentorship about being a healthy pack, they would get into all kinds of relational trouble and likely cause some destruction too. This same phenomenon applies to any human group. Families, teams, classrooms, friend groups, and communities all need a feedback system and boundaries to help everyone know how to work within the culture norms.

Common Misconceptions and Myths About Boundaries

Boundaries got a bad name along the way, perhaps because the term has become saturated in self-help literature. When you hear the word, you think of the "tough love" interventions associated with rock-bottom addiction. For most people, boundaries sound like a firm "no" or look like estrangement in relationships. We talk about setting boundaries as if we draw a line in the sand one day and everything changes. Further, the most common references to boundaries make them sound punitive, final, and extreme. Yet the practice of boundaries is far more nuanced than that. It helps to think about a new relationship as a ball of clay. For it to become an object with shape and intention like a sculpture, you have to mold it. You don't say "no" to the clay. Rather, you move it in different directions in order to create the shape that you want or like. Boundaries in relationships are our most important tool for shaping relationships.

An Important Note About Safety

Sometimes boundaries need to be as firm as a brick wall. When it comes to our psychological and/or physical safety and well-being, our boundaries need to be much more radical. We remove ourselves from situations or people who interfere with our freedoms. The definition of a victim is a person whose choices have been taken away. This is nonnegotiable and is not about shaping relationships but instead about ending them. There are times when we experiment with boundaries and discover that those who we are negotiating with are not willing to participate in the process. People like this have their own brick wall boundaries, and if we continue trying to shape the relationship, it's the equivalent of running face-first into a brick wall. It hurts! And we are more likely to injure ourselves trying to change it.

Humans Are Herd Animals

All mammal groups communicate and negotiate needs on a daily basis. It's an intimate process of knowing each other so we can need each other. Interdependence, the practice of needing each other and sharing resources, allows groups to be more resilient and increases the chances of survival. It's also a great way to conserve energy.

Humans have moved far away from this style of living. We have forgotten how to need each other or how to need each other well. We have to let people in and truly know us if we want them to care about our needs. This is the only way we can grow trust, and it must begin with an individual leap of faith in order to build something that can become strong and sustainable for the greater good.

I've included a graphic that shows trust as a cycle in order to illustrate it as a generative process rather than a fixed destination.

We have to let others know exactly what is happening within us if we want them to be compassionate and/or supportive. We open up so that others might connect to our feelings and empathize. It's the best chance we have to get our needs met. Listening to each other is how we share resources and balance needs.

COURAGE TO CHANGE
The desire to create something new OR the need to respond to pressure and/or pain.

CONFIDENCE IN SELF
The resilience of surviving powerful risks builds emotional muscle.

LEAP OF FAITH
The willingness to uncomfortably move forward without knowing the outcome.

POSITIVE RELATING
Open and honest feedback ultimately reduces pressure and stress and allows relationships to feel more "real" and safe.

VULNERABILITY
Finding the strength to move past fear in order to be transparent and share the truth openly.

AUTHENTIC CONNECTION
The experience of being seen and known for who we really are.

Making Space for Everyone to Play a Role

In the rest of the animal kingdom, mammals negotiate needs all day long. Animal groups are in a constant feedback loop so that they can attend to ever-changing needs. Humans are the same. We need to create an open feedback system that allows us to share resources and balance needs. There are days when we need space and quiet. There are days when we need companionship and lots of compassion. There are times of the day when we have little to offer to others. There are phases of life when we have so much to give. Open communication about our needs allows us to figure out, on any given day, how we can balance our needs. Boundaries are the basic tool or relational skill we use to do this.

Here is the most basic communication that allows us to be clear about our needs, to identify our roles, and to know how we can be of service in our relationships or groups:

Here is what I have to offer _____.
Here is where I need support _____.

When we let people know our needs and what we are doing to care for ourselves, it gives them a chance to support us, to be of service, and to adjust themselves so there is space for you in the relationship. It also introduces a new dynamic in the relationship. As we learn and model a new normal, it can inspire others to consider their needs and take better care of themselves. Be sure to ask others what they need and listen carefully so that you might find a way to support or adjust the relationship.

Real-World Examples of Boundaries and Sharing Needs

- You give your children and partner clear direction and tasks that allow the whole family to be part of the morning routine. This gives everyone a sense of place and purpose in the family.
- A family communicates and makes space for everyone (including you) to have their needs met (social, rest, exercise, etc.). This allows all members to feel they are contributing to the care of each other. This builds empathy.
- Your friend has been doing most of the talking and you most of the supporting. You interrupt and ask your friend to listen to your struggles and to share the friendship space. In doing so, you allow that person to support you and to feel needed by you too.
- You let a manager know that you have too heavy a workload and have a problem you are struggling to solve. They are able to mentor and guide you. This is an honor and privilege for people who are in leadership roles.

How to Build Trustworthy Relationships

Quite a few of the essential building blocks for building trust with others focus on your own inner state and your behavior. It's so important to remember that trust begins with being trustworthy. When we slow down and get ourselves grounded, we are much more trusting of our self-leadership, and we provide that stable emotional mammal for others to connect with. Here are some practical things you can do to build trust with yourself and others:

- **Check Yourself Before You Wreck Yourself.** Take a cue from the 1990s rapper Ice Cube who gives us a great reminder. Do you have ego, anger, anxiety, or baggage that you are carrying into the conversation or relationship? If so, clean up your side of the street so that you are not adding fuel to the fire. Take a moment to sit quietly and leave your ego out of your leadership. If you are struggling with this, seek help and mentorship so you can be a reliable leader. Stable leadership begins with you.
- **Communicate the Context.** Be sure you know the story about how you arrived at this conversation. Be sure to say out loud your intent and purpose. Also, be sure to say a few words about why we give feedback and how it is a practice to help build relationships and help others to grow and develop professionally.
- **Attend to Psychological Safety.** Check in periodically with how others are doing. Simply pausing or slowing down to care can make all the difference in establishing trust and a sense of kinship. It's not your job to act as a therapist or a parent; however, noticing when someone is in distress and naming it gently is often enough to help someone feel safe and to settle down.

- **Stay in the Present.** Keep the conversation focused on matters at hand in the moment. Resist your own urge or others' invitations to revisit things from the past.
- **Keep it Simple.** When talking through difficult subjects that are potentially triggering, it's best to keep topics manageable in size and scope. We can only deliver and receive so much when we are also working on our emotional stability.
- **Be Kind and Humane.** At the end of the day, we're all humans doing the best we can. Stay connected to your own humanity and the hearts and spirits of others. This is a reminder to be gentle with yourself and to speak with kindness. Just this simple awareness can make a difference in how challenging feedback is received.
- **Make a Plan.** It helps to build trust when we discuss next steps. This creates a sense of safety for others and accountability for how we are going to attend to the problems at hand, as well as to the relationship.

The Practice: The Boundary Cycle

Boundary practices begin inside of us. The first and perhaps most important step is to carve out a mindset or inquiry about our own needs. When we allow thoughts of guilt, shame, or focus on others to interrupt our self-inquiry, we can't get to the truth about what we need. Use the Needs Inventory or the Pressure Audit as guides to help you identify needs.

This first step of this practice is about creating a mental space—a moment of curiosity—that we protect and guard so we can identify how to take care of ourselves.

1. Give yourself a moment. Really, about one minute. If you're super practical and you like structure, you can even set a timer!

2. Tune in to your body. Put your hand on your heart. Tune in to your breath. Really allow for an exhale. If it feels good to linger in this step, feel free. It's wonderful to give yourself a few moments of body connection.

3. Imagine that you are standing at a door, and you aren't allowing anyone through. This is what you are going to do with your mind. This is your moment to be with you. Only you. No "should-ing" on yourself. No asking about others' needs. No perfectionism. No expectations. No judgment. This is a moment just for you. For you to be raw and real and simple about what you want and/or need.

4. Ask yourself the question: "What is the simple thing I need/want today?"

5. As you sit with the question, use your body as a guide. It knows. Is it movement or rest? Is it alone time or connection? Does it want to create or receive?

6. Say it out loud in one sentence. "Today, I need/want_____ for me."

7. Lengthen your spine. Sit up straight. Engage your core muscles. Feel your pelvic floor. Plant your feet. Look straight ahead. Shoulders back. Heart open. Wake it all up!

8. Say your one sentence out loud again. This is what it sounds like to own our needs.

Now that you are clear about your needs, take yourself through the Boundary Cycle so that you can get a feel of the process. Remember, this is going to feel awkward and cumbersome at first. You might think that this has way too many steps! But the more you practice, the more intuitive it becomes. Use the Boundary Cycle as step-by-step guide for how to work with your needs, communicate and negotiate with others, and shape and teach some new things in your relationships.

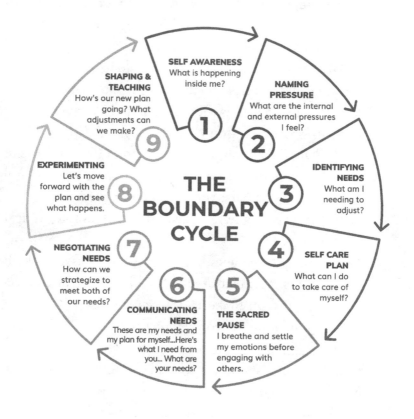

Real-World Example to Use as a Template

Let's use a real-world parenting example to illustrate. This example can apply to any kind of relationship. It's more about the flow of the boundary process than the topic itself. Also, keep in mind that parents are teachers to their children; however, in life and in adult relationships, we are teaching each other all the time. This is the function of boundaries.

Kids interrupt. A lot! They have minimal impulse control and lack awareness of others' needs. Developmentally, this is entirely normal. Practically, it's torture. As a parent, when you are trying to talk, work, think, breathe, your kids walk all over the moment and insert themselves with their questions, demands, chatter, and even their bodies. Kids are experts at physically flooding us with their thrashing arms, pounding feet, and spontaneous full-speed attacks of love. This is a complete assault on our nervous systems. We take it for so long and then reach a tipping point. Usually, our intolerance matches their developmental availability. They are ready to learn a new skill right about the time when we can't take another moment of the behavior.

1. Communicate the need: Tell the child how the interruption impacts you. Truly open up and let them know what it's like. "I want to talk about interrupting. It's really hard on my brain when I'm trying to focus or think and then you interrupt." Ask the child what it's like to hear this. Also, ask if it's hard for them to wait and be patient when they are excited. Learn about interrupting from their point of view.

2. Navigate needs: Explain to the child that this is a life lesson that we all have to learn and you're going to work on it together. No shame or blame. Normalize the lesson. Also let them know that this is an important social life skill. They will want to be good at waiting their turn. No one appreciates people who bulldoze their way through relational experiences.

3. Shaping and teaching. Find a way to talk about the lesson in shorthand. Give it a name, like "reading the room," and walk them through how to be more aware when they

enter a new space. You are teaching them to observe what is happening and what it looks like when there is a lull or an opening. Give them some coping skills for waiting. You might need to brainstorm what they can do when they have to wait. You might do a practice session and role-play what it's like to wait. When children are quite young, they can only wait a short while. But that capacity can grow, especially if we give them the opportunity to grow it. Boundaries are just that: an opportunity for them to learn and grow. With some shortcut language and a practice session, you have a way of shaping the relationship as the interrupting happens.

CHAPTER TEN

Herd

We are all caught in a network of inescapable mutuality, tied into a single garment of destiny. Whatever affects one directly, affects all indirectly. We are made to live together because of the interrelated structure of reality.
MARTIN LUTHER KING, JR.

Whether we think of ourselves as biological creatures or spiritual beings or both, the truth remains: we were created in and for a complex ecology of relatedness, and without it we wither and die.
PARKER PALMER

Learning how to live in the greatest peace, partnership, and brotherhood with all men and women, of whatever description, is a moving and fascinating adventure.
BILL W.

The Story: Mareadise

I'm sitting at the foot of my bed, knees to my chest, looking at the expansive oak tree in the backyard. The gnarled branches and crinkled leaves mirror my internal world. I can hear my own words as they come out of my mouth—my tone and my long pauses—all of it, just lingering in my head. I've begun to annoy myself. Really, I've grown tired of my own story. Like I'm writing the book and I don't like the plot or the characters, but I keep writing it. The phone is pressed against my cheek and sweat beads up on my skin as I listen to my friend take a long breath before asking a very important question. "Beth, do you have any friends?" At first, it seems like a ridiculous question because the person asking *is* a friend. But it lands, and I consider it. She's more of a colleague. I've kept it like that, a layer of professionalism between us. But she just barged right through that layer and asked the question. And now it's mine.

"Of course I do!" I answered.

"Really? Because it seems like you don't. Like maybe you don't really let anyone in," she pushed back, not very gently.

I had just started spending more time with a group of women who I knew through the horses. They came to mind.

"I have friends, Margee. Aren't you a friend?" I asked.

"I supposed so, but you don't really let me support you," she said.

"I have dozens of friends. Friends from childhood. Friends from college," I could hear my own defensiveness.

That phone call happened during the months before I stopped drinking. I was at my loneliest. I wasn't drinking every day or even every week. But I wanted to drink. And, when I did drink, I overdid it. In many ways, I had been hiding. Even from myself. I didn't know I was lonely. I didn't know I was undersupported. There was so much I didn't know. But that call began to uncover a fundamental crisis in my life. That one question exposed a piece of truth I couldn't avoid. I was surrounded by people, yet I didn't allow any of them to get close to me. I held the stories of others, but no one held mine. Physician Dr. Gabor Maté writes about this, "The addict's reliance on the drug to reawaken her dulled feelings is no adolescent caprice. The dullness itself is a consequence of an emotional malfunction not of her making: the internal shutdown of vulnerability." Riddled with guilt and shame and confusion, I didn't want anyone to see me. I only knew how to trust my animals. I had yet to make the bridge to the human herd.

It's thirteen years later, and I'm sitting in the magic corner of the ranch, the spot where all beings are drawn to gather. My horse herd has chosen it as their favorite spot for sleeping. They gather under a magnificent eucalyptus we call The Napping Tree. It's also the corner where we built a large labyrinth, the same design as the one in the cathedral in Chartres, France.

It's the corner where we've held weekly meditation groups led by our beloved neighbors, the Dhammakaya monks from Thailand. They appeared four years ago, standing at the front gate of the ranch, a row of orange robes and smiling faces, a bag of carrots, and an eagerness to teach. After touring the whole ranch, they chose this corner. Of course. The corner chose them. I've learned how to sit still in this corner, to accept my own skin, to settle my mind back into my body so that it can rest and quiet.

This special corner of the world, my world, glows with the evening sun weaving in and out of the trees before it dips behind the hills. The sky is full of golden light, narrow beams shining on the old fence posts. My beloved dog, Glen, rolls onto his back and delights in the feel of the ground. He shimmies his body and snorts and groans. Then he stands up and looks my way. Our eyes meet. He walks over and smiles, puts his head in my lap, and I lay my hand on his muzzle. "Little boy. You're the sweetest little boy." Glen has been on the ranch journey with me every step of the way. He has been my most trusted and steady ally and has allowed me to lean on him while I've taken so many exhilarating risks.

Tonight, the corner is full of women. We sit on benches or on the ground. Some of us huddle under blankets and hold mugs of warm tea or coffee. We talk. We listen. We laugh. We weep. We tell the truth about our inner lives. The corner holds all of us and all of what we need to say out loud. After twelve years of sobriety and hundreds of hours, maybe thousands, of practicing, I know how to do this now. I made a decision to wake up and to recover, to walk through the whole range of human experience and emotion without running, hiding, or numbing. And I learned how to do this by asking for help and accepting it. I know how to let the corner hold me. I know how to let the women hold me. The horses have made their way to the corner. It isn't time for The Napping Tree, so they deliberate along the fence. They are drawn to our human herd, and they join us.

The growth of my horse herd has paralleled that of my human herd. Now there is a family. A matriarchal family. Mares set the herd culture and hold everyone to it. Their commitment to stability and community is everything. I live with them so I can learn with them. I call it Mareadise. It is alive and ever-changing, one moving body consisting of many parts. The herd is the most beautiful and powerful thing I know.

We've recently brought a new member into the herd, a wild mustang. I had dreamt of a mustang adoption since I was twenty years old when I camped among the wild herd in the Superstition Mountains of Arizona. I would stay up all night waiting for them to come to the Salt River to wade about and drink. They took their time in the cool water, and I could watch them with the moonlight showing only their silhouettes. It never seemed like the right time or phase of life to take on such an epic project. Until it did seem right. Until it seemed necessary.

From the Maverick-Medicine herd in Northeastern Nevada, the dun-colored mare and a few hundred other mustangs were gathered by the Bureau of Land Management, separated from their herd members, and put into a holding facility in Idaho. This is the fate of thousands of wild horses who live out their days in those pens. Others become eligible for adoption. This mare, #4109, had a special look in her eye. I knew to trust what I noticed. She was the one.

She had never been handled by humans, so they loaded her into my trailer through a series of chutes. The door of the trailer swung shut, the papers were signed, and she was in my care. The day before I left to pick up the mustang, a friend Sarah asked me, "What's going to happen? You're going to get this wild horse! And then what?"

"I have no idea," I told her, "I really have no idea what is going to happen."

"That's the bravest thing I've ever heard," she said.

I thought about that conversation as I drove the twelve hours back home. Sarah's words stuck. Why was my approach so surprising or extraordinary to her? As I stayed with her comments, I realized my horse herd and the exceptional herd of humans had become my support system, had taught me to live without fear. I really didn't have a plan for the mustang. Sure, I had read some things. But I wanted to stay open and approach it with less of my own agenda. I wanted to practice not knowing what to do. I had learned to trust myself, to trust my human herd, to trust my horses. I knew to listen and to watch, to pay attention, to ask for

help when I needed it. I had spent these years in recovery healing wounds and transforming traumas into resources. The tools
of recovery taught me how to take inventory, to self-reflect, to
allow others to give me honest feedback, and how to course correct or repair when needed. I had come into a deep and unwav-
ering acceptance of my own needs, and I knew how to do those
daily adjustments to return to ease and to peace of mind. I knew
to allow for a natural pace. I knew to listen to my instincts.

Of all the herd member integrations, the wild horse has been
the most powerful. A blank slate. She really was wild, an energy
and aliveness in her body that was electric. I imagined she would
be scared and that I would wait for her fear to subside. But in
those first hours on the ranch, I saw and felt a fully intact being, a
force of self-preservation. She was not afraid. No, it was me who
was afraid. I had no idea I'd be so unnerved by her wholeness.

My herd was entirely intrigued with this new addition. Once
we got her neck tag off, I had the privilege and honor of giving her
a name: Feather. I've been finding feathers for years, and they've
always carried important messages. I found one the day before I
met this mare. The message that day was about what I would need
to access inside of myself as I embarked on the adventure with
this horse. Something light and soft. One feather. But also, part of
something larger and powerful. A wing.

People say you have to keep the wild horses in a separate pen,
and you can't allow them to mingle with your other horses or
you'll never get a relationship going. People say that you have to
get them halter trained and leading before you let them out of
their holding pen. People say that you can't let the mustangs out
into a big pasture, or you'll never catch them. People say a lot of
things about these horses, and those messages registered, for sure.
But in those early days and weeks with Feather, I listened to her

needs. The thing about wild horses is that their sense of self-preservation is much stronger and more developed than a domesticated horse. They will insist their needs are met. They push back.
If you decide to start a dispute, they'll lean into the conflict. I
sensed, in every cell of my body, that I didn't want to start a fight
with this wild horse.

Feather's needs were clear. She needed a herd. Of course she
did. She had lost her family when she was chased by helicopters
and trapped into government trailers. So, I started the process of
introducing her to my herd. Moonshine and Feather fell instantly
in love. It took me a minute to trust her with him. He has been
my baby, after all. But I realized I needed to trust him, and he saw
a friendship from the moment he laid eyes on her. Moonshine and
Riva became her ambassadors. I kept them close by so that she was
never alone.

The rest of the herd took a bit longer. I ran into a dilemma. I
knew that the herd needed as much space as possible so they could
work out their relationships. If there is conflict, the horses ask for
space from each other. In smaller pens, there isn't enough space for
them to get relief from the pressure and this is often how injuries
happen. All of the stories about letting mustangs into pasture ran
through my head. I still didn't have Feather halter trained. I could
approach her and groom her, and she would follow me around. I
could herd her into different areas, and we had established a calm
and peaceful feedback system. I sensed that she needed the space
and the herd in order to fully settle. If she was going to see me as a
reliable herd member, a partner, or even a leader, it was imperative
that I attend to her needs rather than get in the way of them.

After a week or two, the writing was on the wall. She had spent
time with all members of the herd. They had visited her pen or
shared a fence line with her. But it was time to open the gate and

give her all the space she needed. I just knew it was the next right thing to do. Moonshine was nearby, as usual. So, with no fanfare or drama, I just opened the gate. Feather slowly made her way to the opening. She dropped her head to the ground and sniffed the grass. She was calm and peaceful, her golden eyelashes batting slowly as she scanned the pasture. She walked out, stopped, and turned back toward me, walking through the gate and back into the pen.

I was totally puzzled. Did she want me to go with her? I stroked her neck and we breathed together. Yes, she did. It was an invitation. We walked through the gate together and off we went, exploring the pasture and joining the rest of the horses who were calmly grazing near the creek. Feather was becoming part of the herd, her new family. Giving her the space and freedom to join the herd was the most powerful act of love and trust I could provide. This was her most fundamental need. As the days and weeks went by, she found her place in the group. The herd changed shape to accommodate her. It was a constant conversation, micromoments of feedback stitched together into the fabric of family. I stayed in the center of the herd, joined the conversation, listening to their needs, to Feather's needs, sharing my own. This is how we grow trust, how it deepens. We stay together. We stay moving and communicating. We adjust and adapt as things change. But we stay together. No matter what, we stay.

The Concept: Commitment and Interdependence

Let's review. Natural Leadership is our innate capacity to use our instincts and awareness to take care of ourselves and to genuinely and wholly connect with others so that we can live in thriving and effective communities. With our mammal signals informing us of our own needs and the needs of others, we can have a more balanced mindset, and this makes us better able to create and engage with healthy and stable human herds. We use our Natural Leadership to create relational systems that allow us to share resources, to navigate needs, and to negotiate spatial proximity. We are herd animals.

At the heart of all mammal groups, there is a commitment to self-care and an honest negotiation of needs in order to remain a group. Humans are often so lost in our stories of conflict that we miss this very basic but important element of how to stay grounded as individuals while also getting along with others. The most functional relationship systems, small or large, operate with interdependence as a central force. Systems in the natural world are great examples of interdependence. Seeds of some plants can become attached to the fur of animals. When the animals move from one location to another, the seeds of the plant also become deposited in the new location. Interdependence allows for the sharing of resources.

What Are Resources?

Though our intellectual and creative endeavors continue to evolve and flourish, at the end of the day, we are still rooted in our basic needs and the allocation of resources. Each of us has internal resources that make up our strengths and act as sources of resilience. These consist of our temperament, inherent leadership gifts, genetic attributes, education, physical health and strength, emotional fortitude, intelligence, lived experiences, connection to our instincts, and wisdom gained from life challenges. All of these internal resources can be offered as contributions to others and to groups. External resources in the mammal world include safety, shelter, food, water, connection and companionship, belonging, space, proximity, rest, and freedom to move. Humans have more complex subcategories of external resources. Interdependence in groups allows for the sharing and negotiating of both internal and external resources. *Resourcing* is a term that comes out of trauma-informed or trauma-focused care and mental health. It's a process that helps us access our strengths and positive memories so we can tap into the goodness of life and access our resilience when times get tough. Resourcing is a practice. It helps us build and expand an internal capacity. The practice is like focusing on a muscle group in order to better support an area of our body and become stronger. It's very common for us to have more strength and resilience than we are aware of. In fact, the practice of resourcing is often a hugely affirming process that builds our self-esteem and changes our view of ourselves and our capabilities. We discover our gifts and see how they have been serving us all along.

Key Elements of Interdependence

In order for a group to practice interdependence, each individual must know their own unique role and contribution to the greater good of the group. The first channel of Natural Leadership Awareness allows us to know ourselves and our own needs. This is an essential part of being a herd member. Radical self-care allows each member to play their role in sharing awareness in the group so that rest can rotate. This is an ongoing commitment that all herd members maintain. Finally, to sustain a culture of interdependence, mentoring and teaching must occur at all stages of the life cycle. We continue to play active roles as learners and teachers in interdependent groups.

Herd Mind

As changes in the environment occur, an interdependent group mobilizes and attends to those changes as a unit. A mammal group that is in sync can move together in unity and cohesion. There are hundreds of examples of this in the animal world and fewer in the human world. Some great human templates exist in medical teams, first responders, sports teams, and the military. These groups create an interdependent system and practice herd mind in order to gain mastery. When the stakes are high, such as they are in these groups, the incentive to get good at herd mind is a great motivator. The same principles and practices can be applied in other human groups such as families, classrooms, and work teams. But the key to herd mind is practice.

HERD MIND

PRESSURE INCREASES
A change or something new enters the system.

RESPOND
Individuals notice pressure and signal the group.

GATHER AND MOVE
Herd moves until release of pressure occurs.

ASSESS
Herd evaluates for safety.

CHOOSE
Herd decides the next right thing.

SETTLE
Nervous systems regulate.

RETURN TO EASE
Herd returns to calm alert state.

Herd Roles

Animal groups share leadership roles depending on what the group needs at any given moment. Each member's temperament or innate gifts matter in the group and serve a function for the health of all. Animal groups and human herds have natural culture leaders, protectors or warriors, nurturers, jesters, resters, mobilizers, etc. Leadership of the group shifts as needs of the group change throughout the day or the season. Our human groups are typically constructed with a tactical mindset, yet we are missing attention to relational roles. It's common to see human groups without a strong culture leader even though there is a named "leader" in terms of a hierarchy. We see this in corporate teams and classrooms all the time. Emotional and relational leaders help keep the group out of trouble or they know how to get a group through trouble when it does arise. Mammals do not get to live with an infinite sense of safety; however, we can settle and stabilize with a sense that our groups can face adversity together.

Safety and Stability are Created Through Behavior

The bond created in a mammal group allows the members to feel like they are a part of a community. Packs and herds are families. They rely on each other for everything. Though dynamics may change, and feedback may be used to adjust to the ever-changing needs of the group, there is an underlying sense of safety in the group, which was created through ongoing behaviors that build trust and commitment. We put a group of humans together and call them a team, but it doesn't mean that the human herd feels safe. In fact, because of the lack of open communication and feedback, most of our groups are brittle and will snap when under more pressure than normal. So much of our human drama comes after months or years of unaddressed underlying problems. In order to create safety, we need more genuine connection with each other, more opportunities to see and know those in our group and to let them know us. Psychological safety, as evidenced in the most recent research, is the single most important factor in determining a highly effective human team. It really is that simple, and yet it's the last thing we create.

We Need Each Other

Your human herd is your core support system. It consists of the people whose judgment you trust and who will give you honest feedback and guidance. Our herd provides the sense of community we all need. Humans are herd animals, and we have always relied on community to be more resilient. For thousands of years, we have shared resources and leaned on each other. But for a few generations now, we have become quite self-sufficient and have developed habits that have diminished our practices of giving and receiving support. Relying on others does not make us weak. Quite the opposite is true. Interdependency makes us stronger and more resilient. Therapist Esther Perel writes about this, "The extended family, the community, and religion may indeed have limited our freedom, sexual and otherwise, but in return they offered us a much-needed sense of belonging. For generations, these traditional institutions provided order, meaning, continuity, and social support. Dismantling them has left us with more choices and fewer restrictions than ever. We are freer, but also more alone."

We Are Undersupported

As we do an inventory of our support system and the many areas of our personal and professional lives, we often find we are undersupported. This fundamental part of our humanity has to be consciously relearned. We can focus on:

- Identifying trustworthy support
- Asking for specific help
- Letting go and receiving support and care
- Being gentle and kind with ourselves for needing others

Letting others support us allows them to be part of our lives, to participate, to be useful, to experience competency and purpose, and to be of service. People can feel they matter to us. This is an honor. Expressing needs can be a vulnerable experience because there is always a chance that we will not have those needs met or that someone may judge us. But letting people in to support us can deepen our relationships and enrich our lives.

Mentorship

Mentorship is a fundamental practice of all animal groups. For human animals and other highly social mammals, teaching and coaching are essential for building necessary competencies. When we take on the role of coaching or mentoring, we help to galvanize a group culture. By passing along the behavioral traits and social norms, the next generation can adapt and learn. Mentoring keeps us sharp in our practice of social norms, which leads to greater accountability and commitment to the culture of which we are a part. Because of our human ego and generations of hierarchical culture with power imbalances, the human approach to coaching and mentorship tends to stray from a pure intention. We are prone to abuse our influence and interfere with a natural balance of teaching and learning that promotes autonomy and empowerment in others. It's nearly a habit to interfere with others' learning processes and to slow down or block development. This happens when we control or manage instead of facilitating growth.

If you think about it, no other animal group raises their young without a radical commitment to competency and survival. It's not in our best interest, as a species, to interfere with others' learning. Yet we do it all the time!

When a relational system is out of balance, teaching or coaching loses its traction and becomes less effective or entirely impossible. The good news is that our survival instincts will often motivate us to block those who impede our growth. Our brain is wired to feel good about learning and about becoming fit for survival. We get dopamine and serotonin from developing core competencies. We know when a mentorship relationship feels good because our brain and body tell us so. We can familiarize ourselves with the qualities and characteristics of mentorship so we can stay grounded in how we approach coaching and how we allow others to coach us.

Balancing Commitments to Self and Herd

When we consider the concept of commitment, we often think of loyalty to others or our vows in relationships. In the human world, we typically do this first. We commit to others before we are clear about our commitments to ourselves. But in reality, commitment in the external aspects of our lives begins with an inner commitment—the ways that we are true to ourselves, whole in our values and actions, and living in our integrity. We give up, drop the ball, or change course because we don't trust and/or believe that we can handle the challenges, pains, failures, or unexpected outcomes that are part of life. We hit the rough patches and quit. We don't trust ourselves. This causes the light to dim inside of us. We go forward with the always-present ache that we have let ourselves down. This is how our self-esteem weakens. Yet, when and if we take risks, we can ask our fearful egos to fasten their seat belts and prepare for the wild ride of uncertainty.

With support and a plan, we can stay wholeheartedly connected to what we want and begin to take steps to bring those dreams, desires, and plans into concrete reality. As we follow through and move forward, we build trust in ourselves. We begin to believe that we can live with any outcome, handle adversity, and find our way through whatever comes our way. This is how our resilience expands and develops. It is at this point that we are able to more freely and authentically give of ourselves to others. A more supported herd member is able to support others. This is a dynamic phenomenon, a process of balancing needs all day, every day. It's a great opportunity to practice the Natural Leadership Awareness Channels in order to help us work toward a state of balance.

How to Find Your Human Herd

You can create your own virtual herd of humans. You probably already have quite a few people in your herd. It's common, however, that your support people are underutilized or that there are holes in your system that need to be filled. You want to get clear about all areas of your life so you can be thorough about the support you need.

In our personal and professional lives, these are some of the areas in which we need guidance, development, mentorship, advice, and coaching:

- Career development and advancement
- Technical skills growth
- Leadership and relationships
- Organization and productivity

In our personal lives, these are some of the areas in which we need support:

- Marriage/partnership
- Parenting and extended family
- Household management
- Spirituality
- Creativity/style
- Physical wellness
- Finances
- Travel, socialization, recreation, fulfillment

Some people like to make a chart or a list to have a visual representation of their herd. It helps to put pen to paper in order to become more active in the process of committing to your needs. When you feel ready or brave, begin to have some conversations and let the people in your support system know that you consider them part of your herd. Let them know how they support you. If it's someone new, ask them if they are available to support you. This can feel a bit awkward or even a bit formal. We aren't used to such an overt ask. It is a brave action and brings with it an intimacy and a sense of vulnerability.

The more we ask for help and support, the more connected we feel to others. And the more spacious our lives become. This can feel confusing at first. We actually have more freedom when we are supported. Expect more moments of peace and stability. More moments of awe and wonderment. More connection and creativity. More moments of joy and hope.

The Practice: Learning to Need Others

"I'm fine."

"Oh, I'll be okay."

"I don't want to be a bother."

"I just need to spend some more time thinking about it."

"I'll figure it out."

These are some of the things we say to ourselves or to others when we are in denial of our own needs. Denial of needs is one of the most dangerous human habits, and it seems that the more advanced our societies become, the worse this problem becomes. The further away we are from basic survival, the more we lose our awareness for our basic needs. While this can have huge consequences on an individual's well-being, it also has ramifications in human groups. Remember, in an animal group, an individual who isn't getting their needs met isn't able to serve the group and becomes a liability. Just think of a horse who wouldn't allow the other horses to keep watch while he slept. He would be tired and unable to keep up with the herd. If he was closest to a source of danger, he might not notice because of his exhaustion. This could put the whole herd at risk.

Self-sufficiency and independence are greatly valued in highly industrialized cultures. So, we need to practice leaning on each other for support, even in small ways. Try this practice for a few days, preferably a whole week if you can.

1. At the start of each day, take a look at your calendar. Break the day into three sections: morning, afternoon, evening.
2. As you look at each section of the day, think about where and when you might need some help, support, or connection. For instance, if you are used to doing a lot of

the morning routine in your home, find a few things to delegate to others. In your work role, look for at least one person who you can ask for advice, or pick a colleague who can look at your work and give you feedback. If you have a partner or spouse, ask that person for a hug or to listen to your day. These are just a few examples.

3. Write down your ideas on a sticky note and take it with you for the day as a reminder. You can also set a calendar alert throughout the day to help you remember.

4. As you try this, notice what thoughts you have about asking for support. Are you afraid to be a burden? Pay attention to pressure in your body. Do you hold tension anywhere? Also, note what emotions emerge as you experiment with this. Do you feel shame or embarrassment?

5. After you have done this for several days, look back at your calendar and spend some time reflecting. Did it get any easier to ask for help? Did you start to enjoy the connection?

6. Try to identify the areas in which you most benefited and see if you can continue the practice.

Finally, flip the practice and see if you can offer help and support a few times per day. Remember, interdependence is a two-way street, and all herd members contribute to the greater good.

The Drop-Off

The car slows to a stop as we wait for the ranch gate to swing open. I notice the pause feels longer than usual. It's been a harried morning. Not quite frantic, but we were certainly busy-bodied and working with a time crunch we've forgotten how to manage. We've been home for a year, crawling through the unfamiliar and traumatic landscape of a global pandemic. We've moved through the iterations of isolation as our community, and the world, shut down, then clumsily but in earnest tried to reopen and create a way of living alongside COVID-19, a mysterious and ever-changing threat to our old way of life. Today, Emma will go back to in-person school, and I will work without interruption for the first time in a year. One year. One very challenging year.

The trimmings of our household privilege have been more evident than ever. Even with most of our routines and infrastructures stripped away, we have stayed conscious of our resources and our luxuries. It's like a song of gratitude has become the background music of our days. It's always going through our heads and sometimes we sing the words. *Thank goodness for this. We're lucky for that. We are so fortunate.* We've continued to have so many of our needs met. Healthy food. Fresh water. Stable housing. Healthcare.

198 | THE HUMAN HERD

Mental healthcare. Financial security. A mostly safe community. Loving family. Outdoor activity. Our serene ranch. The animals. We've had so much.

Yet we've been aware of a pervasive and enduring hardship. We have carried uncertainties and unknowns for longer than the human mind is used to handling them. Though many cultures face ongoing trauma due to war, poverty, famine, racism, religious persecution, and other attacks on humanity, many of us are not equipped to cope with this much change or with such a prolonged loss of freedom. We don't know how to do this. We've been writing the story as we go. We are living and breathing a psychological thriller, one day at a time.

Things have happened around us and to us. Schools closed. Stores closed. Towns closed. We were told to stay home, to keep a distance from each other, to fear each other, to wash everything, wear masks. People have gotten sick. So many have died. Hospital systems reached beyond capacity. Jobs disappeared. Financial systems crashed. Supply chains broke. Grocery shelves gathered dust instead of food. Families have tried to work, to parent, and to provide education to our children. Women, in particular, have felt a disproportionate amount of this impossible load, and it continues to affect our careers and our health.

We have shared many of the same pandemic pains, but each of us had our own unique narrative of suffering. With an inflamed global system and our fears heightened, our more primitive mammal instincts have gone into high alert. In a state of survival and scarcity, we are more focused on differences, more guarding of resources and territory. We've become rigid in our thinking, brittle in our emotional reactions, and violent with our bodies. We have fought over everything: race, gender, politics, healthcare, education, science.

In our more local realm, the usual cooperation of parents and schools deteriorated into anger and intolerance. My client work slowed nearly to a stop. Our California ranch became surrounded by wildfires and was under a curtain of heavy smoke for months. Our local synagogue was defaced with anti-Semitic graffiti. Riots in nearby cities had us on high alert. Within our home, our only-child household felt the loneliness and quiet of zero playdates or online learning. Anxiety and depression symptoms surfaced. The pressures and longstanding issues of a twenty-year marriage became clearer than they had ever been. A divorce happened. Our family ended.

As we pause at the gate, I notice that it can't open fast enough. I have an urgency to leave. I can feel it in my skin. I'm visualizing the drop-off, the moment when Emma gets out of the car, closes the door, walks away, and I am alone. We've been mostly quiet on the drive. I'm preoccupied with thoughts about work and how I'm going to fit as much as I can into the three hours Emma is at school. It's a hybrid learning experiment with some kids online and some in the classroom. It was hastily planned and there was very little communication about the details. But I signed up immediately, knowing that our mental health was just as important as our physical health. Today my mind and body are out in the future, and it feels like I'm driving a getaway car.

We make the last turn and head into the parking lot where the drop-off system now involves health screening questions and temperature checks. I feel something shift, the air in the car almost thickening. Emotional pressure can fill a space. I look at Emma, and her eyes are full of worry and tears. "What is it, sweet girl?" The tears start to flow as I ask the question. It's the question of awareness. Something is happening, and we need to observe it out loud. This is how we live and breathe. This is how we relate and love. She doesn't know how to answer. Because she is ten years old. And because she is full of emotion. But we stay with the question. "Are you feeling nervous about school?" I ask. I've hit the mark. The sobbing begins. I can feel the pressure in the car release. The tightness in my own chest softens. I've been tense too. I tell her this, "Right! Of course. We are both feeling this today. This is a huge change. We've been together for a year. At home."

She nods her head, but then it seems that she's holding something back. I can feel it because the flow between stops a bit. It's subtle, but she looks away from me. It's a signal. I pull the car over so we can stay with the moment, so we can slow things down. She tells me she's fine and directs me to carry on and drive toward the drop-off lane. Her voice is rushed and full of stress. I steer the car toward a parking spot. I slow us way down so we can stay with the awareness. "Do you know what else is making you nervous?" I ask her. She shakes her head and continues to cry. I haven't been supporting her this morning. I've been in my head, focused on my needs, dead set on my pace, my agenda.

I take one really good deep breath, and almost immediately, my scope is back. It's like I'm standing on the hilltop, and I can see the big picture. This drop-off is a big deal. She needs support. Of course. She has forgotten how to get dropped off. She has lost the skill. Her childhood development carried on, her emotional and intellectual capacities expanding in so many directions, while at the same time, the world stopped, and she had very little opportunity to play with new parts of herself. All of her growth had been happening in the bubble of home. Sheltered in place. She hadn't had ongoing practice with things like school drop-off so that it could be integrated along the way. What other social and emotional behaviors have regressed or stopped developing? What other skills has she forgotten? What confidences has she lost? What is it like to be a child of a pandemic shutdown?

"It's been so long since you've gone to school that it probably feels like you forgot how to do it."

"Yes, Mommy. Yes! That's exactly it."

"Let's take it slow. We can sit here as long as you need to."

I think about how different the school looks with all of the COVID protocols—how everyone's faces are masked, and how odd and frightening it must be for a child to navigate the world wanting safety, yet the world has become ridden with danger, full of signals that our environment isn't safe. I put my hand on her arm and meet her eyes. I give her a light squeeze.

"I know it feels unfamiliar to be at school and so many things are different here. But I feel safe about you going to school," I tell her.

"You do?" she asks with huge surprise.

"Yes, I wouldn't send you if I didn't think it was safe."

"Really?" she asks.

"Really. And everyone here is feeling this. You aren't alone. This is a big change for everyone."

Now we have trust flowing between us. It's like we released a tourniquet. The fast-paced morning with too much pressure and not enough communication caused an interruption of our relational blood flow. It's back now, and a sense of ease is emerging. Our connection is creating solid ground for Emma. I can feel her standing on it. I can feel myself there too. Once again, this wise being has slowed us down. She has allowed her very real inner experience to surface so those around her can know and feel what is happening. She has told the truth. Her truth. But she has also expressed a universal truth. She has illuminated an unmet need, shined her brilliant light on precisely what needs to be seen.

This has been a profound trauma for the human herd. How are we going to heal this? How are we going to find a state of ease in an environment with so much dis-ease? It helps to slow down and allow for natural transitions, to leave space so we can settle and allow our systems to come into balance and to return to ease. It helps when we admit that we have needs. It helps when we ask the world around us to listen. It helps when we are seen, when we are held. It helps when we accompany each other through these difficult moments or days or months when things feel impossibly painful or frightening or heartbreaking. It helps when we find fellow travelers to walk alongside as we face the hard things together. It helps when we have a herd.

ABOUT THE AUTHOR

Beth Anstandig is changing the way organizations, leaders, and individuals use their power. As a lifelong cowgirl, writer, professor, and licensed psychotherapist, Beth has twenty-five years of experience developing, implementing, and training people in Natural Leadership—a model she pioneered. Beth owns Take a Chance Ranch in Morgan  Hill, California where she provides leadership, culture, and well-being programs through The Circle Up Experience. She's trained thousands of leaders and teams from some of the most renowned corporations, universities, and nonprofits.

Beth's fresh perspective and work integrating basic animal practices into everyday human life have been featured in global media, including BBC World Service, PBS, and *Forbes*. She is a frequent podcast guest, contributing writer for MomsRising, and an advisor and content creator for Kahilla: A Basecamp for Women on the Rise.

Beth has an M.A. degree in Counseling Psychology from Santa Clara University and an M.F.A. degree in Creative Writing from Arizona State University. She lives on her ranch with an expanding community of animal herds.

A free ebook edition is available with the purchase of this book.

To claim your free ebook edition:

1. Visit MorganJamesBOGO.com
2. Sign your name CLEARLY in the space
3. Complete the form and submit a photo of the entire copyright page
4. You or your friend can download the ebook to your preferred device

Print & Digital Together Forever.

Snap a photo

Free ebook

Read anywhere

CPSIA information can be obtained
at www.ICGtesting.com
Printed in the USA
JSHW041305110722
27978JS00001B/38